THE BOOK OF
SENIOR JOKES

Also published by Michael O'Mara Books:

The Book of Senior Moments by Shelley Klein

More Senior Moments (The ones we forgot . . .) by Shelley Klein

You Know You're Past It When . . . by Shelley Klein

The Seniors' Survival Guide by Geoff Tibballs

THE BOOK OF SENIOR JOKES

(The Ones You Can Remember)

Geoff Tibballs

MICHAEL O'MARA BOOKS LIMITED

First published in Great Britain in 2009 by
Michael O'Mara Books Limited
9 Lion Yard
Tremadoc Road
London SW4 7NQ

A CIP catalogue record for this book is available from the British Library.

Papers used by Michael O'Mara Books Limited are natural, recyclable products
made from wood grown in sustainable forests. The manufacturing processes
conform to the environmental regulations of the country of origin.

ISBN: 978–1–84317–399–1

    4 5 6 7 8 9 10

www.mombooks.com

Designed and typeset by Design 23

Printed and bound in Great Britain by Clays Ltd, St Ives plc

INTRODUCTION

Apart from an afternoon nap, a comfy chair and a nice cup of tea and a biscuit, we seniors enjoy nothing more than a good laugh . . . which is why what may appear to the uninitiated to be wrinkles on our faces are actually laughter lines. This brings to mind an exchange between the late George Melly and Mick Jagger. Melly asked Jagger, whose face could best be described as 'lived-in': 'How come you've got more lines on your face than me?' Jagger cheerfully replied that they were laughter lines. To which Melly retorted caustically, 'Surely nothing's *that* funny.'

It is an accepted fact that laughter keeps us feeling young – after all, Bob Hope and George Burns both lived to be a hundred whereas Karl Marx, who probably never told a decent joke in his life, only made it to sixty-four. And let's face it, so many things in life are sent to try us seniors that we have to see the funny side. When kindly teenagers offer to help us across the road even though we have only just turned forty, or when we sink our teeth into a nice juicy steak and they stay there, what else can we do except laugh? Laughter really is the best medicine – unless you've got something like pleurisy when antibiotics are possibly a safer bet.

Nor do we mind being the butt of jokes. We know all the senior stereotypes – absent-minded, doddery, incontinent, sex starved – but we also know through years of experience that the ability to laugh at ourselves is priceless. But be warned: the art of joke telling becomes more difficult with age. There was a good reason why Bob Hope had cue cards placed strategically around the stage – it was to remind him what came next. As our minds inevitably grow more befuddled with the passing years, our joke-telling skills can deteriorate embarrassingly. We sometimes become so confused that we start a joke with the punchline; or forget key points in the story and have to add a lengthy explanation at the end; or even attach the wrong punchline to the joke.

'My dog's got no nose.'

'How does he smell?'

'No, she went of her own accord.'

So if you're worried about sounding more like George Bush than George Burns, simply read out selected jokes from this collection to your friends and family. You never know, after months of practice you may even be able to remember their names.

Resourceful Wife

Two old ladies met in the supermarket. After inquiring about each other's health, the conversation turned to their respective husbands.

'Oh,' said one, 'Bert died last week. He went out to the garden to dig up a cabbage for dinner, had a heart attack and dropped dead in the middle of the vegetable patch.'

'Oh, my!' exclaimed the other. 'What did you do?'

'Came here to buy a cabbage.'

The Face Looks Familiar

An elderly couple were driving across the north of England. The woman was driving when they got pulled over by the police.

'Excuse me, madam,' said the officer, 'did you know you were speeding?'

The woman, who was hard of hearing, turned to her husband and asked, 'What did he say?'

'HE – SAYS – YOU – WERE – SPEEDING,' the old man said loudly and slowly.

'May I see your licence?' asked the officer.

The woman again turned to her husband. 'What did he say?' she asked.

'HE – WANTS – TO – SEE – YOUR – LICENCE,' the old man said.

The woman gave the officer her licence. The policeman examined it and, as he handed it back, remarked, 'I see you are from Glasgow. I spent some time there once and went on a blind date with the ugliest woman I've ever seen.'

The woman turned to her husband and asked, 'What did he say?'

'HE – THINKS – HE – KNOWS – YOU!'

Standing by the Wife

An old woman was arrested for shoplifting in a supermarket. When she appeared in court, the judge asked what she had taken.

'A tin of peaches,' she said.

'Why did you take it?'

'They looked ever so nice,' the old woman answered. 'Fancied them for me tea but didn't have any money.'

The judge thought for a bit. 'Well, in view of your years I am prepared to be lenient. How many peaches were in the tin?'

'Four,' answered the old woman.

'Right – that will be four days in jail, one for each peach. Court dismi—'

'Your honour?' an old man cried.

'Yes?'

'My wife also stole a tin of peas.'

Marriage Proposal

An elderly widow and a widower had been dating for seven years. After much indecision, he finally summoned up the courage to ask her to marry him and she immediately said 'yes'. But the following morning he couldn't remember what her answer had been, so, in a state of mild panic, he decided to call her.

'This is really embarrassing,' he said, 'but when I asked you to marry me yesterday, well, this morning I simply couldn't remember what your answer was.'

'Thank goodness you called,' she replied. 'I remembered saying "yes" to someone's marriage proposal, but I couldn't remember who it was!'

Age Concerns

Three little old ladies were sitting around discussing the problems of ageing. The first lady said, 'You know, I'm getting really forgetful. This morning I was standing at the bottom of the stairs and I couldn't remember if I was just about to go up or if I had just come down.'

'Oh, that's nothing,' said the second lady. 'The other day I was sitting on the edge of my bed, wondering if I was going to bed or if I had just got up.'

'I'm pleased to say my memory is as good as ever, touch wood,' said the third lady, rapping her knuckles on the table. Then remarked: 'That must be the door – I'll get it.'

Virility Test

A couple in their late seventies decided to consult a fertility expert to see whether it was possible for them to have another child. The doctor said that recent scientific developments had greatly improved the prospects, but he was unwilling to commit himself until the husband had provided a semen sample. So he gave them a jar to take home and asked them to return in the next day or two with the sample.

Two days later, they went back to the doctor's with an empty jar.

The husband apologized profusely. 'I tried my right hand,' he told the doctor, 'and then I tried my left hand. My wife tried her right hand, and then she tried her left hand. She even took her teeth out and used her mouth. But still we couldn't get the lid off the jar.'

A Problem Solved

A farmer had had to walk to the nearby town to collect supplies for his smallholding as his car had broken down. He called in at the hardware shop to pick up a bucket and an anvil, then he stopped by the livestock dealer to buy a couple of chickens and a goose. With no means of transport, he was faced with the problem of how to carry all his purchases home, but the livestock dealer had a good idea. 'Why don't you put the anvil in the bucket, carry the bucket in one hand, put a chicken under each arm and carry the goose in your other hand?' he suggested.

'Yes – that works. Thank you,' said the farmer, and off he went. He had barely walked ten minutes when he bumped into a little old lady who told him she was lost.

'I need to find a house called The Laurels,' she said. 'Do you know it?'

'Indeed I do,' said the farmer. 'As a matter of fact, it's on the way to my farm, so I can show you if you like.'

'How far is it?' asked the old lady.

'Only five minutes if we take a short cut down this alley.'

'But,' said the old lady, 'how do I know that when we get in the alley, you won't pin me against the wall, pull up my skirt, and have your wicked way with me?'

'Good grief, woman!' exclaimed the farmer. 'In case you hadn't noticed, I'm carrying a bucket, an anvil, two chickens, and a goose. How in the world could I possibly pin you against the wall and have my wicked way with you?'

The old lady replied, 'Put the goose down, put the bucket over her, and the anvil on top of the bucket, and I'll hold the chickens.'

A Moving Experience

An absent-minded academic had just moved to a new house further along the same street. All too aware of his tendency to forget things, his wife took the precaution of writing down the new address on a piece of paper before he set off for work that morning. 'Here's the key to our new house,' she said, 'and remember, don't come back here this evening, go to the new address.'

'Very well, dear,' he replied, and set off for work.

Inevitably in the course of the day he mislaid the slip of paper and, forgetting all about the move, he automatically returned to the old address. When he tried the key, he couldn't get in. This prompted him to remember the move and to search in his pockets for the piece of paper, which was nowhere to be found.

In desperation, he wandered along the street and stopped the first approachable young man he came across.

'Excuse me, young man, I'm Professor Richardson. You wouldn't happen to know where I live, would you?'

The boy sighed. 'Come with me, Dad,' he said.

Stage Fright

A theatre usher was alarmed to see an elderly gentleman crawling on his hands and knees beneath a row of auditorium seats in the middle of a serious dramatic play.

'What are you doing, sir?' he whispered. 'You're disturbing the audience around you!'

'I've lost my gum,' answered the old man, continuing to search under the seats.

'Sir,' continued the usher, 'if that's your only problem, allow me to offer you another stick of gum so that you can sit down and watch the rest of the play. A stick of gum is not worth all this commotion.'

'But you don't understand,' said the old man. 'My false teeth are in that gum!'

Hearing Loss

Two elderly gentlemen were sitting down to breakfast. One said to the other, 'Do you know you've got a suppository in your right ear?'

'Speak up. I can't hear you. My hearing aid is not working,' the other man bellowed.

The first man tapped his ear and pointed to his companion, who delved in his ear.

'Ah?' said he, removing the suppository. 'I'm glad you pointed that out. Now I think I know where I put my hearing aid.'

Drink Driving?

Ruby, who lived in a nursing home, was confined to a wheelchair although she was otherwise physically strong and active. She was, however, two sandwiches short of a full picnic.

Every night, when most of her fellow residents had retired to their rooms for the night, she would whizz around the nursing home in her electric wheelchair, making car noises.

'Brrm, brrmm . . .' she was driving her car along a corridor, making squealing-tyre noises as she took a turn far too fast. 'Beep, beep!' she would shout, waking up anyone who had actually managed to fall asleep. Some of the residents were annoyed, but most of them had got used to Ruby's driving antics and were amused by them; some joined in.

As she hurtled round a corner one night, Colin stepped out and raised his hand. 'Stop!' She stopped. 'May I see your driving licence, please, madam?' Ruby delved in her bag and produced a small diary which she handed to him: 'Here you are, officer.' Colin took the diary, flicked through it and handed it back, and off she drove, just as Doris stepped up to her saying, 'You can't park here, madam.'

As she drove down the next corridor, Phil came out of his room and called, 'Stop!' He leaned down to her as she came to a halt. 'Your left-hand headlight seems faulty, madam. Did you know this?'

'Oh no, officer, the lights were working perfectly when I set off.'

'Well, may I see the vehicle's documentation?' Ruby dug in her bag once again and this time produced a sheaf of old medication notes, which she handed to Phil. He made a play of examining the papers, handed them back and sent her on her way.

She was just approaching Eddie's door when it flew open and he stepped out in front of her, stark naked and in an all too obvious state of arousal. 'Stop!' he cried.

'Oh no,' said Ruby, looking at what was in front of her. 'Not the breathalyser again!'

Turning a Deaf Ear

A husband was becoming increasingly concerned that his wife might have a hearing problem. So as they relaxed watching TV in their favourite armchairs one evening, he called across to her: 'Can you hear me, Ethel?' There was no response.

A few seconds later he asked her again, this time a little louder. 'Can you hear me, Ethel?' Still there was no response.

So he tried for a third time, louder still. 'Can you hear me, Ethel?'

She answered impatiently: 'For the third time, yes!'

Funeral Procession

A middle-aged man was walking along the street when he noticed an unusual funeral procession approaching the cemetery. There was a long black hearse at the front of the procession followed some distance back by a second long black hearse. Behind the second hearse was a solitary man walking with a dog on a lead. Behind him were around two hundred men walking in single file.

Unable to contain his curiosity, the passer-by respectfully approached the man walking the dog and said, 'I am so sorry for your loss, and I realize this is a bad time to disturb you, but I've never seen a funeral like this. Whose funeral is it?'

'My wife's.'

'I am so sorry to hear that. What happened to her?'

'My dog attacked and killed her.'

'Oh no! And who's in the second hearse?' inquired the passer-by.

'My mother-in-law. She was trying to help my wife when the dog turned on her.'

The passer-by thought for a moment, and then asked tentatively, 'May I borrow the dog?'

'Get in line.'

Proof Required

An elderly man went to apply for social security benefit. As proof of his age, the woman behind the desk asked him for his driver's licence but he found that he had left it at home.

'Never mind,' said the clerk, 'unbutton your shirt.'

He thought it a strange request, but nevertheless he opened his shirt to reveal tufts of silver hair.

'That silver hair on your chest is sufficient proof for me,' said the clerk.

Later at home the old man recounted the story to his wife.

She listened patiently before remarking caustically: 'It's a pity you didn't drop your trousers – you might have qualified for disability benefit, too!'

Senior Symptoms

An elderly man went to see his doctor. 'I need your help, doctor,' he said. 'Whenever I make love to my wife, my head starts spinning, my legs go weak at the knees, and I struggle to catch my breath. I'm worried that it could be something serious.'

'Well,' said the doctor, 'I'm afraid symptoms like yours can happen during sex as you get older. Just remind me, how old are you?'

'Eighty-nine.'

'And when did you first notice these symptoms?'

'Three times last night and twice again this morning.'

The Precious Hat

On a day of gale-force winds, a police officer noticed an elderly lady standing by the side of the road, gripping her hat while her skirt blew up around her waist.

He went over to her and said, 'Excuse me, madam, I don't wish to cause you embarrassment, but while you're holding on to your precious hat, passers-by and motorists are getting a good look at everything you have!'

'Listen, son,' she replied. 'What they're looking at is seventy-seven years old. But this hat is brand new!'

Table Manners

Sitting at the dinner table, a daughter complimented her father on his improved manners. 'I'm pleased to see that after all these years you have finally learned to put your hand over your mouth whenever you cough.'

'I have to,' he replied. 'It's the only way I can catch my teeth.'

Putting the Cat Out

A middle-aged couple were going out to the theatre for the evening. They had got ready, donned their best clothes and put the cat out in readiness for the arrival of their taxi. But as the taxi pulled up and they opened the front door, the cat shot back into the house. Knowing from experience that the cat would wreak havoc if left alone in the house, the husband went back in after it while the wife waited in the taxi.

Noticing that there were quite a lot of people apparently just hanging around in the street on this warm summer evening, the wife became nervous, not wanting anyone to work out that the house would be empty for some hours, so she announced loudly – ostensibly to the taxi driver, but for all to hear: 'My husband's just gone in to say goodbye to my mother.'

A few minutes later, the husband re-emerged from the house and got into the taxi.

'Sorry I took so long,' he said. 'The stupid thing was hiding under the bed and I had to poke her with a coat hanger to get her to come out.'

Reason to be Cheerful

A group of pensioners were sitting around in a nursing home comparing their respective ailments.

'My hands are so shaky I can hardly lift this cup,' said one.

'My cataracts are so bad I can't see to pour my coffee,' another said.

'I can't turn my head because of the arthritis in my neck,' said the third.

'My blood pressure pills make me dizzy,' complained the fourth.

'I guess that's the price we pay for getting old,' remarked the fifth.

'Yes, but it's not all bad,' said the sixth comfortingly. 'We should be thankful that we can all still drive.'

Loving Words

A couple who had been married for thirty-five years were lying in a hotel bed. They were just about to go to sleep when through the walls they heard a girl's voice say, 'Oh, honey, you're so strong.'

The husband turned to his wife and asked, 'Why don't you ever say that to me?'

'Because,' she replied, 'you're not strong any more.'

A few minutes later, they heard the girl's voice again: 'Oh, honey, you're so romantic.'

The husband turned to his wife, 'Why don't you ever say that to me?'

'Because,' she answered, 'you're not romantic any more.'

Five minutes later, they heard the girl's voice groan: 'Oh, honey, that was a wonderful orgasm. Thank you.'

The husband turned to his wife: 'Why don't you ever tell me

when you have a wonderful orgasm?'

'Because,' she said, 'you're never around when I have them!'

Absent Friends

A little old lady received a home visit from a church worker who asked her how she was feeling.

'I'm worried sick,' replied the old lady.

'Why's that?' asked the church worker. 'You're in good health, aren't you?'

'Yes.'

'Then why are you so worried?'

'Every close friend I ever had has already died and gone to heaven,' explained the old lady. 'And I'm afraid they'll all be wondering where I went!'

Heart Murmur

An old man went to the doctor for a regular check-up. The doctor listened to his heart and declared: 'I'm afraid you have a serious heart murmur. Do you smoke at all?'

'No, doctor.'

'Do you drink to excess?'

'No, doctor.'

'Do you still have a sex life?'

'Yes, doctor.'

'Well, I'm sorry to have to be the bearer of bad news, but with this heart murmur, you'll have to give up half of your sex life.'

'Which half?' asked the old man, 'the looking or the thinking?'

Seagull Attack

Two old men were sitting in the garden of their nursing home when a seagull flying overhead pooped on the bald head of one of the men.

The nurse who was in attendance said urgently, 'Don't worry, I'll run and fetch some toilet paper.'

As she hurried off, one old man turned to the other: 'Is she crazy or what? By the time she gets back with the toilet paper, that bird will be miles away!'

An Apple a Day

A young man asked a wealthy pensioner how he had made his fortune. The old guy leaned back in his chair and began his story. 'Well, son,' he said, 'it was 1932, the height of the Great Depression, and I was down to my last nickel. I invested that nickel in an apple. I spent the entire day polishing that apple and at the end of the day I sold the apple for ten cents.

'The next morning, I invested those ten cents in two apples. I spent the whole day polishing them and sold them at the end of that day for twenty cents. I continued this system for a month, by the end of which I'd accumulated a fortune of $5.30. Then my wife's father died and left us two million dollars.'

Tasty Peanuts

A boy visited his grandmother with his friend. While the boy was talking to his grandmother in the kitchen, his friend ate peanuts from a dish on the living room table. When it was time to go, he said goodbye to his friend's grandmother and thanked her for the peanuts.

'That's all right,' said the old lady, 'Since I lost my dentures I can only suck the chocolate off 'em!'

False Alarm

An elderly lady called the police to report that her car had been broken into. 'They've stolen the stereo, the steering wheel, the brake pedal, even the accelerator!' she wailed.

The operator replied reassuringly, 'Don't worry, madam, an officer is on his way.'

A few minutes later, the woman called back sheepishly: 'Would you mind telling the officer not to bother. I've just realized I got into the back seat by mistake.'

School Reunion

An elderly man attended a school reunion but was dismayed to find that his surviving classmates simply wanted to talk about their various ailments – heart conditions, liver complaints, kidney stones.

When he arrived back home, his wife asked him how it went. 'It wasn't so much a school reunion,' he sighed, 'more like an organ recital!'

Exercises for Seniors

1. Begin by standing on a comfortable, flat surface, where you have plenty of room at each side. With a 2kg potato bag in each hand, extend your arms straight out from your sides and hold them there as long as you can. Try to hold for a full minute and then relax.
2. Each day, you'll find that you can hold this position for just a bit longer.
3. After a couple of weeks, move up to a 5kg potato bag.
4. Then try a 25kg potato bag and eventually try getting to the stage where you can lift a 50kg potato bag in each hand and hold your arms straight for more than a full minute.
5. When you feel confident at that level, try putting a potato in each of the bags.

Memory Test

Three senior men were at the doctor's for a memory test. 'What is two times two?' the doctor asked the first.

'177,' came the reply.

Then the doctor asked the second old man: 'What is two times two?'

'Wednesday,' the man said.

The doctor then turned to the third old man and asked him: 'What is two times two?'

'Four,' he answered.

'That's excellent,' enthused the doctor. 'How did you get that?'

'Easy,' said the third old man. 'I subtracted 177 from Wednesday.'

Leg Pain

An elderly man went to his doctor to complain about a pain he had been feeling in his left leg. The doctor examined the leg thoroughly but could find nothing wrong. In the end he said, 'You probably won't want to hear this, but I think the pain in your left leg is simply the result of old age.'

'Your diagnosis can't possibly be correct,' said the patient haughtily. 'After all, my right leg is perfectly okay.'

'What does your right leg have to do with it?' rapped the doctor.

'Well, my right leg doesn't hurt at all and it's exactly the same age!'

Sleepless Nights

A man in his sixties said to his wife: 'I think it's time we tried for another baby.'

'Are you crazy?' she said. 'Have you forgotten what it was like, all those sleepless nights? How would we cope with it at our age?'

'Yes,' he said, 'I know I used to complain about getting up at two o'clock in the morning to feed the baby, but these days I usually have to get up around that time anyway!'

Final Request

A London widow decided to prepare her will and make her final requests. She told her solicitor that she wanted to be cremated and that she wanted her ashes to be scattered all over Selfridges.

'Why Selfridges?' asked the solicitor.

'Because,' she replied, 'that way I can be sure my daughters will visit me twice a week.'

A Grim Outlook

A middle-aged woman accompanied her husband on his annual medical check-up. Afterwards the doctor took her to one side and said, 'I'm afraid I have some bad news. Unless you follow a strict routine, your husband will die. Every morning, you must give him a good healthy breakfast and in the evening you must cook him a nutritional meal. You mustn't burden him with any household chores, you must keep the house spotless and you must attend to his every need. I realize it will mean extra work for you, but it really is the only way to keep him alive.'

On their way home, the husband asked his wife what the doctor had said to her. 'Oh,' she replied. 'He said you're going to die.'

The Naked Truth

Jerry and Bill were sitting in the lounge of their nursing home when one of the female residents suddenly ran past stark naked.

'Was that Doris?' asked Jerry.

'I couldn't be too sure,' replied Bill. 'My eyesight's not so good these days.'

'Neither is mine,' agreed Jerry. 'What do you think she was wearing?'

'I don't know,' said Bill. 'But it sure needed ironing.'

Careless Driving

Two elderly ladies were out driving in a big car. Both women were so small that they could barely see over the dashboard. When they came to a junction, they went straight through even though the light was red. 'I must be losing my mind. I could have sworn we just went through a red light,' the woman in the passenger seat said to herself.

A few hundred yards along the road, they came to another junction, and once again they sailed through on a red light. The woman in the passenger seat looked uneasily at her friend but still said nothing.

Shortly afterwards they went through yet another red light. This last violation was too much for the woman in the passenger seat who could hold her tongue no longer. 'Ada!' she said. 'Don't you realize we just went through three red lights? You could have got us into serious trouble – or even killed!'

'Oh,' said Ada. 'Am *I* driving?'

A Golfer's Wisdom

A young man was just about to start a round of golf when an elderly gentleman walked over to ask if he could join him. Despite misgivings that the older player might slow him down, the younger one agreed.

To his surprise and delight, the old man was a quick player. He only ever hit his drives about 150 yards but he was no slouch along the fairways.

Eventually they reached the tenth hole, where the younger player hooked his drive into a plantation, leaving himself with a tall pine tree standing between his ball and the green. Seeing his opponent's predicament, the old man volunteered, 'When I was your age, I used to hit the ball right over that tree to the green.'

Without stopping to think, so eager was he to show off his skills, the young man took an almighty swing at the ball and then watched in horror as it thudded into the tree trunk and rebounded twenty yards behind him.

The old man remained silent for a few seconds before remarking: 'Of course, when I was your age that pine tree was only three feet tall.'

Cosmetic Surgery

A fifty-five-year-old woman was walking along the road when she heard a voice from above boom out: 'You will live to be one hundred.'

That must be the voice of God, she thought to herself; that means I have another forty-five years left.

So she went off to see a cosmetic surgeon and had everything fixed from head to toe – face lift, breast implants, tummy tuck, the complete works. But then as she left hospital after the extensive surgery, she was hit by a bus and killed.

Up in Heaven, she berated God: 'You told me I would live up to be a hundred. That meant I had another forty-five years. Why did you let that bus kill me?'

'Sorry,' said God, 'I didn't recognize you.'

Anniversary Celebration

Two men were chatting in a bar. 'Isn't it your fiftieth wedding anniversary soon?' asked one of them.
'Yes, it is,' said the other.
'And are you going to do anything special to celebrate?'
'Well, for our twenty-fifth anniversary, I took my wife to Australia. So maybe for our fiftieth I'll go and fetch her.'

The Sound of Silence

A wise old gentleman retired and bought a modest home near a junior high school. The first few weeks of his retirement were peaceful and content . . . until the new school year started. Then, every weekday afternoon, three exuberant schoolchildren took great delight in noisily beating every rubbish-bin lid they encountered on their way home from school. After enduring two weeks of this, the old man decided to take action.

The next afternoon he walked out to meet the young percussionists as they banged their way down the street. Stopping them, he said, 'I like what you kids do. I used to do much the same when I was your age. You've got life, you've got rhythm. In fact I'm so impressed that I'd like to give you a dollar each if you promise to play those bin lids every day.'

The kids could hardly believe their luck, and for the next few days they joyously played the bin lids, creating a fearful noise all the way down the street. Then one afternoon the old man greeted them again, but this time he wore a solemn expression.

'Kids,' he said, 'the recession's really putting a big dent in my income. From now on, I'm afraid I'll only be able to pay you 50 pence to drum on the bins.'

The youngsters were clearly displeased, but they grudgingly accepted the reduced rate and continued their afternoon ruckus.

A few days later, the wily old man approached them again as they drummed their way down the street. 'Listen,' he said, 'I haven't received my pension yet this month, so I'm not going to be able to give you more than 25 pence. Will that be okay?'

'A lousy 25p?' sneered the drum leader. 'If you think we're going to waste our time drumming these bins for that, you're crazy! No way, mister. We quit!'

And the old man enjoyed peace and tranquillity for the rest of his days.

Word Association

A church minister decided to try something a little different for his Sunday sermon. He told his congregation: 'I am going to call out a single word, and I want you to sing a hymn that immediately springs to mind.'

First, the minister shouted out: 'Cross.'

And the congregation started to sing in unison 'The Old Rugged Cross.'

Next he shouted out: 'Grace.'

And the congregation immediately burst into a rendition of 'Amazing Grace.'

Then the minister called out: 'Sex.'

There was a stunned silence from the congregation with everyone looking at each other nervously until a little old lady at the back started to sing in a frail, trembling voice: 'Precious memories . . .'

Trip of a Lifetime

A travel agent looked up from his desk and noticed an elderly man and an elderly woman eyeing the posters of glamorous destinations in his shop window. From their sad expressions he could tell they were unable to afford any of the holidays on offer, but because business was booming he decided on an unprecedented act of generosity. Calling them into his office, he told them: 'I realize that on your pension you could never hope to stay at a five-star hotel, but I'm offering you exactly that – for free! Two weeks in a luxury hotel in the Bahamas, all paid for by me. It's my good deed for the year.'

'That's so sweet of you,' said the old lady, and the pair happily accepted the kind gesture and left with their tickets.

A month later, the old lady was passing by the shop when the travel agent spotted her. 'How did you enjoy your holiday?' he called out.

'Oh, it was wonderful,' she said. 'The flight, the hotel, everything was first-class. Thank you so much. Just one thing puzzled me, though. Who was that old guy I had to share the room with?'

High-School Crush

On a first visit to her new dentist, a middle-aged woman noticed his diploma on the wall. Reading his full name, she remembered a boy of the same name on whom she had a major crush in high school. Could it be the same person? she wondered excitedly.

Her eager anticipation evaporated the moment she walked into his room. For there before her stood a balding, grey-haired man with a wrinkled face. Surely he was way too old to have been her classmate, but to satisfy her curiosity she asked him if he had attended Sycamore High School.

'Yes, I did,' he replied.

'What year did you graduate?' she asked.

'1966,' he said.

'I was there then!' she exclaimed.

'Really?' he said. 'What did you teach?'

Impatient Patient

An elderly man was admitted to hospital for the first time in his life. As he toyed with the bell cord which had been connected to his bed, he asked his son, 'What's this thing?'

'It's a bell,' replied the son.

The old man then pulled it three times. 'I can't hear it ringing,' he said.

'No,' explained the son, 'it doesn't ring. It switches on a light in the hall for the nurse.'

The old man was highly indignant. 'If the nurse wants a light on in the hall, she can damn well switch it on herself!'

Mark of Respect

Two men in their sixties were playing golf one day at their local course. One of them was about to chip on to the green when he saw a long funeral procession on the road running alongside the golf course. He immediately stopped in mid-swing, removed his cap, closed his eyes and bowed his head in prayer.

'That was a most sensitive to do,' his playing partner said afterwards. 'You really are a very considerate man.'

'Well, I was married to her for thirty-seven years.'

Fatal Medication

A woman went to the doctor to get some medication for her elderly husband. The doctor said: 'I want him to take two of these pills every Saturday, Sunday and Monday and skip the remaining days in the week.'

A month later, the woman returned to inform the doctor that her husband had died of a heart attack.

'I don't understand it,' said the doctor. 'He had no history of heart problems. I hope it wasn't a side effect of the medication.'

'Oh no,' said the wife. 'The pills were fine. It was the skipping that killed him.'

Unexpected Pleasure

After nearly forty-five years of marriage, a couple were lying in bed one evening when the wife felt her husband start to fondle her in an unusually passionate manner. His right hand started at her neck and then made its way down her back, his fingers exploring every fold of skin. He then switched to the front, tenderly caressing her breasts before stopping at her lower stomach. Next he gently brushed her left buttock and placed his hand on her left inner thigh, moving down to feel her calf. Then he transferred his hand to her other leg, proceeding up her inner thigh until he reached the very top of her leg. Suddenly without warning he stopped and moved his hand away.

As she had become quite aroused by this caressing, she said lovingly, 'Darling, that was wonderful. Why did you stop?'

'I found the remote,' he mumbled.

Doctor's Orders

At her annual medical check-up, an elderly lady was told by the doctor that in order to improve her heart rate, she should try to indulge in sexual activity three times a week. Embarrassed, she asked the doctor to repeat the suggestion to her husband.

So the doctor went into the waiting room, took the husband to one side and told him that his wife needed sex three times a week.

'Which days?' inquired the husband.

'Well, something like Mondays, Wednesdays and Fridays would be ideal,' said the doctor.

'Okay, doctor,' said the husband, 'I can get her here Mondays and Wednesdays, but Fridays she'll have to take a taxi.'

The Trials of Golf

A group of men in their seventies were playing a fourball game of golf. As they trudged around the course on a particularly cold day, they started to feel their age.

One said, 'These hills are too steep for my old legs.'

The second complained, 'And the bunkers are too deep.'

The third moaned, 'And it's hard work walking through this thick rough.'

'Be grateful,' said the fourth. 'At least we're still on the right side of the grass!'

A Wonderful Life

After living a colourful life, an ageing gigolo finally found that the years were catching up with him. So he went to the doctor for a check-up.

'I've had a lifetime of wine, women and song,' he boasted, 'and I don't think I'd be able to give it all up.'

'Well, the good news,' said the doctor, 'is that you won't have to give up singing.'

Jewish Confession

An old man went into confession. 'Father, I'm eighty-two, married with seven children and fifteen grandchildren,' he told the priest. 'Last night I strayed and made love to two nineteen-year-old girls. Twice.'

'I see,' said the priest. 'And when was the last time you were in confession?'

'Never, Father,' replied the old man. 'I'm Jewish.'

'Then why are you telling me?'

'I'm telling everybody!'

The Delayed Divorce

A couple in their late eighties appeared before a judge to seek a divorce. 'He gambles, he drinks too much and he chases women. I've had enough,' the wife moaned.

'She doesn't do any housework, she's a lousy cook and she sleeps around,' the husband countered

'How long has all this been going on?' asked the judge.

'About seventy years,' they replied in unison.

'The judge was puzzled. 'So why have you waited until now to get a divorce?'

They said: 'We were waiting for the kids to die.'

Sleeping Pills

A woman was visiting her elderly father in a nursing home. He seemed brighter than usual and told her: 'I've been sleeping really well lately. I think it's the new medication they've been giving me.'

'What's that, then?' asked the daughter.

'Well, every night they give me a glass of warm milk and a Viagra tablet.'

'Viagra!' exclaimed the daughter. 'Why are they giving you that?'

'I don't know,' said the old man.

On her way out, the daughter asked a nurse about the new sleeping aids.

'The warm milk helps him sleep,' explained the nurse.

'Yes, I understand that, but what's the Viagra for?'

'Oh,' said the nurse, 'that's to stop him rolling out of bed.'

Breaking the Habit

Two senior citizens were discussing their respective husbands over a cup of tea. One said, 'I wish I could get Alf to stop biting his nails. It's such a revolting habit.'

Her friend said, 'My Leonard used to do the same. But I managed to cure him of the habit.'

'Oh, do tell me. What's your secret?'

'I hid his teeth!'

No Milk Today

A doctor entered his examining room to find a woman and baby waiting for him. After examining the baby, the doctor revealed that he was concerned that it wasn't gaining enough weight. 'Is the baby breast-fed or bottle-fed?' he asked.

'Breast-fed,' replied the woman.

The doctor ordered the woman to strip down to her waist and

he then proceeded to knead and pinch both of her breasts. Motioning her to get dressed, he said, 'No wonder this baby is hungry. You don't have any milk.'

'I know,' she said. 'I'm his grandmother. But I'm glad I came!'

Water, Water Everywhere

A lady walked into a bar on a cruise ship and ordered a scotch with two drops of water. As the bartender poured it, she revealed that it was her eightieth birthday.

Hearing this, a fellow passenger offered to buy her a drink. 'Thank you,' she said. 'How kind. I'll have another scotch with two drops of water.'

The bartender was impressed by her drinking capacity but was mystified why each time she asked for just two drops of water in her whisky.

'Well,' she explained, 'when you've reached my age, you've learned how to hold your liquor. But water is a different matter!'

A Room with No View

An elderly lady from the country was visiting the city for the first time in her life. She checked in at a five-star hotel and let the porter take her bags. She followed him, but as the door closed, her face fell in disgust.

'Young man,' she said angrily. 'I may be old and not used to your big city ways, but I'm not stupid. I paid good money for this room and it won't do at all. I expected a darn sight better than this – it's too small and there's no proper ventilation. Hell, there's not even a bed!'

'Madam,' replied the porter, 'this isn't your room, it's the lift!'

Romantic Date

A couple began dating after meeting on a seniors' coach trip. They enjoyed each other's company and after taking things slowly at first, the relationship began to get more physical, and one evening after a romantic candlelit dinner, they ended up in bed together.

Afterwards, each was lost in private thought. He was thinking, 'If I'd known she was a virgin, I'd have been more gentle.'

And she was thinking, 'If I'd known he could still get it up, I'd have taken off my tights.'

Deadly Serious

A wife woke up one morning and leaned over to give her husband an affectionate kiss.

'Don't touch me!' he barked. 'I'm dead.'

'What on earth are you talking about?' she said. 'We're both wide awake. What makes you think you're dead?'

'I must be dead,' he replied, 'because I woke up this morning and nothing hurts!'

Pet Names

A widower was invited round to his friends' house for dinner one evening. He was touched by the way the husband preceded every request to his wife with a term of endearment – 'My love', 'Honey', 'Sweetheart', 'Darling', etc. Even though they had been married for nearly sixty years, they were still clearly very much in love.

While the wife was in the kitchen, the guest leaned over to the husband and said, 'I think it's really sweet that after all the years you've been married, you still call your wife by those pet names.'

'To tell the truth,' replied the husband, 'I forgot her real name about ten years ago.'

Lost in Translation

Three men who were a little hard of hearing were walking along the street on a blustery day.

One said, 'Windy, isn't it?'

'No,' said the second, 'it's Thursday.'

The third man said, 'So am I. Let's have a beer.'

Cruise Tragedy

An elderly couple were on a cruise in the Caribbean when a terrible storm suddenly blew up. As waves lashed the ship, the old woman was washed overboard. A team of divers searched day and night but were unable to find her, so eventually the captain took the old man ashore and promised to notify him as soon as there was any news of his wife.

Three weeks later, the old man received a fax from the ship. It read: 'Sir, sorry to inform you we found your wife dead at the bottom of the ocean. We hauled her up to the deck and attached to her rear end was an oyster and it contained a pearl worth £50.00. Please advise.'

The old man faxed back: 'Send me the pearl and re-bait the trap.'

Crushed Nuts

A little old man shuffled into an ice cream parlour and pulled himself slowly and painfully up on to a stool. After catching his breath, he ordered a banana split.

The waitress asked, 'Crushed nuts?'

'No,' he replied. 'Arthritis.'

A Talking Frog

An eighty-eight-year-old man was out fishing one day when he heard a voice say: 'Pick me up.' He looked around but couldn't see anyone. Then a few moments later, he again heard the voice say: 'Pick me up.' This time he looked down and saw a frog lying on the surface of the water.

'Are you talking to me?' asked the old man.

'Yes,' replied the frog. 'If you pick me up and then kiss me, I will turn into a beautiful, vivacious young woman who will fulfil your every fantasy. I will become your bride and you'll be the envy of all your friends.'

After considering the matter for a minute or two, the old man picked up the frog and put it in his pocket.

The frog cried, 'Why haven't you kissed me? Are you crazy? Didn't you hear what I just said? I can become your beautiful, vivacious young bride!'

'No,' said the old man. 'At my age, I'd rather have a talking frog.'

Charity Visit

The popular singer Tony Bennett paid a charity visit to a care home to cheer up the elderly residents. However he was dismayed that none of the residents appeared to recognize him. Finally in frustration he went up to one old lady and said,'Do you know who I am?'
The old lady whispered: 'Don't worry, dear. Matron will tell you.'

Chat-Up Line

A debonair man in his late eighties visited a classy cocktail lounge where his gaze immediately alighted on an attractive woman some twenty years his junior. Trying to remember his best pick-up line, he asked her, 'Tell me, do I come here often?'

Planning for the Future

A couple in their early seventies were discussing their future plans. The husband asked, 'What will you do if I die before you?'

The wife thought for a moment before replying, 'I will probably look to share a house with three other single or widowed women, maybe people a little younger than me since I am still active for my age. What about you? What will you do if I die first?'

He answered, 'Probably the same.'

Golf in Heaven

Jerry and Dave were golf fanatics. They had played on their local course virtually every day for over fifty years and were still capable players even though both were now well into their seventies. One day Jerry was in a philosophical mood and asked Dave: 'Do you think they play golf in heaven?'

'I don't know,' replied Dave, 'but I guess at our age we might find out before too long.'

Sadly, a week later Dave dropped dead.

Jerry struggled to come to terms with the loss of his friend but six months later he was reading the sports section of the newspaper when the ghost of Dave suddenly appeared before him.

'Is that really you, Dave?' asked Jerry.

'Yes, it's me,' answered Dave. 'I'm in heaven.'

'Great!' exclaimed Jerry. 'I've got to ask you: do they play golf in heaven?'

'Well,' said Dave, 'I have good and bad news on that subject.'

'What's the good news?' asked Jerry.

'The good news,' said Dave, 'is yes, they do play golf in heaven.'

'Okay,' said Jerry, 'so what's the bad news?'

Dave hesitated for a moment before replying: 'The bad news is you have a tee time for tomorrow morning.'

Need for Speed

A retired millionaire bought himself a Mercedes convertible for his seventy-fifth birthday. He was soon driving along a Florida highway, enjoying the sensation of the wind blowing through what little hair he had left on his head. This is the life, he thought; he saw himself leaning elegantly against his car, bikini-clad young ladies hanging round his neck, gazing adoringly into his eyes. He increased his speed to 80 mph, then to 85, to 90 . . . but was that a siren he could hear above the rushing of the wind?

A glance in his rear-view mirror revealed a highway patrol trooper behind him, blue lights flashing, gaining on him. I can get away from him with no problem, thought the man , flooring the pedal so that the car was flying along at 100 mph. The needle crept up to 110, then 120 mph.

What am I doing? he suddenly said to himself. I'm too old for this kind of thing. He pulled over to the side of the road and waited. The trooper pulled in behind the Mercedes, got out of his vehicle and walked up to him. 'Sir,' he said, looking at his watch. 'It's Friday and my shift ends in 20 minutes. If you can give me a reason why you were speeding that I've never heard before, I'll let you go.'

The man looked at the trooper and said, 'Years ago my wife ran off with a Florida State Trooper. I thought you were bringing her back.'

'Sir, have a nice day,' the trooper replied and turned back to his car.

Dating Agency

A man in his sixties joined an online dating agency and began a correspondence with a woman of similar age. Eventually he suggested that they should meet and decided to be completely honest with her from the outset. He wrote, 'I admit I am no oil painting. My entire face is covered in vivid red boils and I have a deep scar running across my forehead. I am 4 foot 11 inches tall, completely bald, I only have one eye, my left shoulder is six inches lower than my right and I walk with a pronounced limp. Meet you in the market square outside the bookshop at noon on Saturday.'

She wrote back: 'I am not concerned about your appearance and am looking forward to meeting you on Saturday. Could you please carry a copy of *The Times* so that I can recognize you.'

Passport to Paradise

Having been married for nearly sixty years, an eighty-five-year-old couple died in a car crash. They had previously been in good health, mainly due to the wife's interest in health food and exercise.

When they reached the pearly gates, St Peter showed them their spacious living quarters – complete with swimming pool and conservatory – and reminded them that because it was Heaven, everything was free. Then he took them around the magnificent golf course and when the husband asked how much it cost to play there, St Peter told them again: 'This is Heaven. Everything is free.'

Next St Peter took them to the restaurant, where a sumptuous buffet was laid out. 'And don't forget, it's all free,' he said.

Trying to take in the magnificence of the spread, the husband asked, 'Is there any low-fat and low-cholesterol food here?'

'You don't have to worry about what you eat here,' said St Peter. 'That's the joy of Heaven! You can eat whatever you want.'

'Damn it, Jessica!' yelled the husband, stamping his foot in a fit of rage. 'If it weren't for your goddamn bran muffins, we could have been here ten years ago!'

What's on the Menu?

An elderly man and a Baptist minister were sitting next to each other in an aeroplane. As the flight had been delayed, the crew announced that passengers would receive complimentary drinks by way of an apology.

When the pretty young flight attendant came round with the drinks trolley, the old man requested a whisky and soda. 'And what would you like?' she then asked the Baptist minister.

'I would rather commit adultery than drink alcohol!' he snapped.

The old man looked confused and, handing his drink back to the attendant, said: 'I'm awfully sorry, I didn't know there was a choice.'

The Wrong Suit

A matter of minutes before her husband's funeral, a grieving widow decided to take one last look at his body. To her horror she saw that he was wearing a brown suit whereas she had specifically told the undertaker that she wanted him buried in a blue suit. She immediately tracked down the undertaker and demanded that the suit be changed. He initially tried to tell her that it was too late for such a change but when he saw that she was not going to back down, he ordered his assistant to wheel the coffin away. A few minutes later, just as the funeral was about to begin, the coffin was wheeled back in and the widow was pleasantly surprised to see that the corpse was now wearing a blue suit.

After the service, the widow made a point of praising the undertaker for his quick work.

'Oh, it was nothing,' he said. 'It so happened that there was another body in the back room and he was already dressed in a blue suit. All we had to do was switch heads.'

Skiing Trip

Two senior gentlemen – Tom and Bill – decided to go on a skiing trip but on their way north their van was halted by a terrible blizzard. So they pulled into a nearby farm and asked the attractive lady who answered the door whether they could possibly stay the night.

'You may stay,' she replied, 'but I am recently widowed and I worry what the neighbours will say if I allow two men to share my house. So I am afraid you will have to sleep in the barn.'

'Don't worry,' they said, 'that's fine by us, and if the weather breaks, we'll be gone at first light.'

The weather did indeed clear in the morning, and they continued their trip north.

Ten months later, Bill received an unexpected letter from an attorney. The next time he saw Tom, he said, 'Do you remember that good-looking widow from the farm we stayed at on our skiing trip last year?'

'Sure,' said Tom.

'While we there, did you happen to get up in the middle of the night, go up to the house and pay her a visit?'

'Well, er, yes, I admit I did,' said Tom, embarrassed at being found out.

'And did you use my name instead of telling her your real name?'

'Yes, buddy, I have to own up. I did. I'm really sorry. Anyway why do you ask?'

'Because she's just died and left me everything.'

Carjacker

An elderly Florida lady returned to her car with her shopping to find four men in the act of leaving with her vehicle. She dropped her shopping bags, drew her handgun, and shouted at the top of her voice, 'I have a gun, and I know how to use it! Get out of the car! The four men didn't wait for a second invitation. They got out and ran for it.

The lady, somewhat shaken, loaded her shopping bags into the back of the car and got into the driver's seat. Her hands were trembling so much that she could not get her key into the ignition. She tried and tried, and then it dawned on her why.

A few minutes later, she found her own car parked nearby. She transferred her bags to it and drove to the police station. The sergeant to whom she told the story could not stop laughing. He pointed to the other end of the counter, where four pale men were reporting a carjacking by a mad, elderly woman described as white, less than five feet tall, glasses, white hair and carrying a large handgun. No charges were filed.

The Henpecked Husband

After more than thirty years of marriage, during which time he had been constantly under his wife's thumb, a husband finally decided to put his foot down and show her who was the boss.

'From now on,' he barked, 'things around here are going to change. I'll be the one giving the orders. You will cook my dinner as and when I want it, you will wash and iron my clothes without complaint, and you will arrange my best clothes on the bed because tonight I am going to the casino with my friends. And who do you think will be buttoning up my shirt and tying my shoelaces?'

The wife looked at him and replied calmly, 'The undertaker.'

Welcome Trespassers

At the bottom of one of his fields an elderly farmer had a large pond, which he had cleaned up, separated from the rest of the farm by high hedges, and set up with a table and benches – a little haven, he thought, to relax in at the end of a long day's hard work during the summer months.

Needless to say, he hardly ever had time to relax and apart from the odd early-morning visit to check the pond and clear away any weed, he never went there. On one of these mornings he was surprised to see a towel spread over the table.

That evening he thought he'd go down to his pond. As he approached he could hear voices shouting and laughing with glee, and he reached his pond to find a group of young women skinny dipping in it. To his disappointment he was soon spotted and, having ascertained he was elderly and not a gorgeous hunk, the young women all sank into the water leaving just their heads above water.

'We're not coming out until you leave,' one of them called to him. 'I didn't come down here to watch you ladies swim or make you get out of the pond naked,' the old man replied, amused. 'I only came down to feed the crocodile.'

Rising Prices

For the first time in many years, a man decided to go to the cinema. After buying his ticket, he stopped at the concession stand to buy some popcorn. Handing the attendant £1.50, he couldn't help but comment: 'The last time I came to the movies, popcorn cost only 30 pence.'

'Well, sir,' replied the attendant with a smile, 'you're really going to enjoy yourself. We have sound now.'

Young Love

A senior citizen walked into an exclusive New York jeweller's with a pretty young woman on his arm. 'I'd like the twenty-four-carat gold necklace in the window,' he announced, 'the one priced at $35,000. Will a cheque be all right?'

'Certainly, sir,' said the sales assistant. 'But we'll have to wait a few days for it to clear. Can you come back on Monday to collect the necklace?'

'Of course,' said the old man, and he and the girl walked out arm-in-arm.

On the Monday the old man returned to the shop, where he was greeted by an irate salesman. 'You've got a damn nerve coming back,' raged the clerk. 'That cheque of yours bounced all the way to Washington!'

'Yes, I'm sorry about that,' said the old man. 'That's why I've come back – to apologize, and to thank you for the best weekend of my life.'

Time to Go Home

A middle-aged man sat at a bar and ordered a double vodka. He drank it, looked inside his jacket pocket and ordered another double vodka. When he had finished that drink, he looked inside his jacket pocket again and ordered yet another double vodka.

Puzzled by this routine, the bartender asked him, 'Why do you look inside your jacket pocket every time you order a drink?'

'I'm looking at a photo of my wife,' replied the man. 'When she starts to look good, I know it's time to go home.'

Like a Baby

Two old men were sitting in the park watching the world go by. One said: 'I don't know about you, but at eighty-four my body is full of aches and pains.'

'Oh, I feel like a newborn baby,' said the other.

'Really?'

'Yes. No teeth, no hair, and I think I've just wet myself.'

Hospital Discharge

A nurse was responsible for discharging patients at a large hospital. She was doing her rounds one day when she noticed an elderly man already dressed and sitting on the bed with a suitcase at his feet. Although he insisted he didn't need any help leaving the building, she pointed out that hospital rules dictated that he should have a wheelchair. Reluctantly, he allowed her to wheel him to the lift.

On the way down, the nurse asked the old man whether his wife was meeting him.

'I don't know,' he replied. 'She's probably still upstairs in the bathroom changing out of her hospital gown.'

Delayed Reaction

'How did it happen?' asked the doctor as he tended a middle-aged farmhand's broken leg.

'Well, doctor, twenty-five years ago . . .'

'Never mind the past,' said the doctor. 'Tell me how you broke your leg this morning.'

'Like I was saying, twenty-five years ago on my first night working on the farm, the farmer's beautiful daughter came into my room and asked me if there was anything I wanted. And I said, "No, everything is fine." She asked whether I was absolutely sure there was nothing she could do for me, and I said, "No, there's nothing."'

'That's all very interesting,' said the doctor impatiently, 'but what has this story got to do with your broken leg?'

'Well, this morning,' the farmhand explained, 'when it finally dawned on me what she meant, I fell off the roof!'

Planning for the Future

An elderly couple had been courting for nearly seven years and finally decided it was time they got married. But first they agreed they should work out the details of how their marriage was going to work in order to avoid any misunderstandings or disappointments.

So over dinner they had a long conversation about their future. They discussed finances, living arrangements, and all manner of things that affected them both. The old man took written notes of every point they covered. Finally he thought he should mention the physical side of their relationship.

'How do you feel about sex?' he asked tentatively, pencil in hand.

'Well,' replied the old lady, choosing her words carefully, 'I'd have to say . . . I would like it infrequently.'

The old man inquired, 'Is that one word or two?'

Child Bride

An eighty-eight-year-old man was undergoing his annual check-up. When asked about his general health, he announced gleefully: 'I've got an eighteen-year-old bride who is pregnant with my child. How about that, doctor?'

The doctor thought for a moment and then said, 'Allow me to tell you a little story. I used to know a man who was a keen hunter, but one day he left home in a hurry and accidentally picked up his umbrella instead of his shotgun. Later that day, he came face to face with a huge grizzly bear. The hunter raised his umbrella, pointed it at the bear and squeezed the handle. And guess what – the bear dropped dead.'

'That's impossible,' said the old man. 'Someone else must have shot that bear.'

'That's kind of what I'm getting at,' said the doctor.

The Hired Hand

An elderly rancher had just married a vivacious girl of twenty-one. His good friend, the town mayor, was concerned about how long the old man would be able to satisfy such a young bride and feared that the marriage might quickly disintegrate. So he advised the rancher to recruit a hired hand to help around the place, knowing full well that the hired hand would probably help out in the bedroom, too, behind the old man's back. To the mayor's relief, the rancher thought it was a great idea.

A few months later, the mayor called on his friend again and asked, 'How's your new wife?'

'She's pregnant,' replied the old man.

The mayor smiled knowingly. 'And how's the hired hand?'

'Oh, she's pregnant, too!'

Pillow Talk

A senior couple were lying in bed one night. He was trying to get some sleep but she was feeling nostalgic and amorous and wanted to talk.

She said, 'You used to hold my hand when we were courting.'

Wearily he reached across, briefly held her hand and then attempted to get back to sleep.

Shortly afterwards she said, 'Then you used to kiss me.'

Mildly irritated, he reached across, gave her a peck on the cheek and settled down to sleep.

A few moments later she said: 'Then you used to bite my neck.'

In a temper he threw back the bedclothes and climbed out of bed.

'Where are you going?' she asked.

'To fetch my teeth!'

Somewhere to Avoid

An elderly man said to his friend: 'I wish I knew where I was going to die.'

'Why would you want to know that?' asked the friend.

'So that I could avoid ever going there!'

Silent but Deadly

An old lady went to the doctor and said, 'I have this really bad flatulence problem, but fortunately there's no stink and no sound.'

'Very well. Take two of these pills every day for two weeks and then come back to see me,' the doctor said:

A week later the old lady returned to the doctor and complained: 'Now, not only do I fart a lot but they smell really bad!'

'Right,' said the doctor. 'Now that we've got your sinuses cleared, let's work on your hearing!'

The Wrong Way

An elderly man was driving along the motorway when his mobile phone rang. It was his wife. 'Arnold,' she said. 'I just heard on the news that there's a car going the wrong way on the motorway. Please be careful.'

'Hell!' exclaimed Arnold. 'It's not just one car. It's hundreds of them!'

Healing Hands

An elderly couple were watching a healing service on TV. The evangelist proclaimed that anyone who wanted to be healed should place one hand on the TV set and the other hand on the affected body part.

Slowly the old lady got to her feet, tottered over to the TV, placed her right hand on the set and her left hand on the arthritic shoulder that had been causing her such pain.

Then the old man got up, made his way over to the TV, placed his right hand on the set and his left hand on his crotch.

'What do you think you're doing?' snapped his wife. 'The idea is to heal the sick, not raise the dead!'

Goodbye, Mother!

A young man was buying a few items at the supermarket when he noticed an elderly lady following him around. Thinking nothing of it, he ignored her but when he reached the checkout, she stepped in front of him.

'Excuse me,' she said, 'I'm sorry if my staring at you has made you feel uncomfortable but it's just that you remind me so much of my son who died recently.'

'I'm sorry to hear of your loss,' said the young man.

'I wonder if you would do something for me?' asked the old lady. 'As I leave the supermarket, would you call out "Goodbye, Mother"? It would make me feel so much better.'

'No problem,' said the young man.

So when the old woman left with her trolley, the young man called out: 'Goodbye, Mother!' Then as he stepped up to the checkout counter, he saw that his bill was £95.90.

'That can't be right!' he told the checkout clerk. 'I only bought a few items.'

The clerk replied, 'Your mother said that you would pay for her.'

Energetic Groom

At the age of eighty-two, Arnold shocked his friends by marrying Emma, a young woman of twenty-nine. She loved him dearly but because of his age, she insisted that they have separate bedrooms on their wedding night in case the exertion proved fatal.

After the reception, they went up to their respective rooms and Emma got undressed and climbed into bed. A few moments later, there was a knock on the door. It was Arnold, ready for action. She let him in, they made love and he then went back to his room while she settled down to sleep.

Ten minutes later, there was another knock on her door. It was Arnold again, and he was ready for more action. Surprised, she consented to sex, and afterwards he bade her goodnight and returned to his room.

Fifteen minutes later, she was woken by another knock on her door. Once again it was Arnold, desperate for sex. Amazed by his prowess, she let him in and they made love. Afterwards she said, 'You're a remarkable man, Arnold. I've been with guys less than a third your age who could only manage it once a night, let alone three times!'

Puzzled, Arnold turned to her and said, 'Was I here before?'

Rare Disease

On a visit to the doctor, an elderly man announced that he was sure he was suffering from a rare tropical disease.

'But if you had that particular disease,' said the doctor, 'you wouldn't actually know because there is no pain or discomfort associated with it.'

'I know,' said the old man, 'and those are exactly my symptoms.'

Death Wish

Shortly before his death, an elderly man instructed his wife:
'When I die, I want you to put all my money into the coffin with
me. I've worked hard to earn that money, and I want to take it to
the afterlife with me.'

So on the day of his funeral, just before the coffin was lowered
into the ground, the wife asked the undertaker to open the lid.

Her friend said, 'Surely you're not going to go along with the
old miser's last request?'

The wife said, 'I am a woman of my word.'

The lid was opened, and the wife pushed in a large envelope,
in accordance with the deceased's wishes.

'You must be crazy!' said the friend.

'I did what I promised,' replied the wife. 'I got all of his money
together, put it in my account and wrote him a cheque. If he can
cash it, he can spend it!'

Fresh Air

On his one hundredth birthday, an old man was visited by a
reporter from his local newspaper.

'How have you managed to live so long?

'Well, young man, when we got married, my wife and I

agreed that if we had arguments the loser would go for a long walk to get over being angry. I was twenty-one at the time – I suppose I have benefited from seventy-nine years of fresh air.'

Age Gap

A man in his eighties was watching a group of teenage girls chatting in the street.

He turned to his friend and said, 'I wish I was twenty years older.'

'Don't you mean twenty years younger?' queried the friend.

'No, twenty years older. Because then I wouldn't give a damn one way or another!'

On the Beach

An elderly couple were sitting on the beach. The old lady turned to her husband and said, 'What do you think of my flip-flops?'

'Act your age,' he replied curtly, 'and put your bikini top back on.'

The Gas Men Cometh

Two gas company employees were making house calls. The younger man decided to wind up his senior colleague by taunting him about his age.

'Maybe I'm no longer in the first flush of youth,' said the older man, 'but I bet I can still outrun you.'

'Right. You're on,' said the younger man. 'How about a race around the block?'

With that, they began running as fast as they could around the block. The two men were neck and neck all the way but as they approached the final corner, they were amazed to see an elderly lady sprinting alongside them.

'What are you doing?' they panted.

She replied, 'Well, you were at my home checking my gas meter, so when I saw you running away, I thought I'd better run, too!'

For Old Times' Sake

Over a romantic anniversary dinner, an elderly couple reminisced about when they first met sixty years earlier. 'Do you remember,' said the husband, 'how on our third date I made love to you against the fence behind the tavern?'

'How could I ever forget?' she smiled.

With a mischievous glint in his eye, he said: 'What do you say we go back there again tonight and recreate the moment for old times' sake?'

'Oh, you are wicked!' she laughed, and grabbed her coat.

Parking their car behind the tavern, the pair tottered gingerly over to the fence with the aid of walking sticks, watched, unbeknownst to them, by an amused police officer in a patrol car. Slowly they stripped from the waist down before she leaned back on the fence and they started making love. Immediately they entered into a frenzy of passion, thrashing around wildly with more energy than a couple a quarter of their age. This went on for more than twenty minutes, at the end of which they both collapsed panting on the ground.

To make sure they had come to no harm, the police officer left his patrol car and went over to talk to them. 'That was amazing!' he said. 'I've never seen such wild, prolonged love-making from two people your age. You must have had a fantastic life together. What's your secret?'

'There's no secret,' gasped the old man, 'except that sixty years ago that damn fence wasn't electrified!'

A Maths Lesson

A middle-aged couple were discussing their future. The husband announced: 'When I'm eighty, I intend to find myself a pretty twenty-year-old girl and have the time of my life.'

'And when I'm eighty,' said the wife, 'I plan on finding myself a twenty-year-old hunk. And as you know, twenty goes into eighty a lot easier than eighty goes into twenty!'

Lifetime Prescription

An elderly man returned from the hospital looking worried.

'What's the matter?' asked his wife.

'The consultant said I have to take one of these tablets every day for the rest of my life,' the husband replied.

'That's not too bad,' said the wife, trying to cheer him up.

'It is,' said the husband. 'He only gave me seven!'

Time for Divorce

An old lady shuffled into a lawyer's office and told him that she wanted to divorce her husband. The lawyer was surprised. 'If you don't mind me asking,' he said, 'exactly how old are you?'

'Eighty-eight,' she replied.

'And how old is your husband?'

'Eighty-nine.'

'How long have you been married?' continued the lawyer.

'Sixty-seven years,' answered the old lady.

'I see,' said the lawyer, scratching his head in bewilderment. 'And why do you want a divorce after so many years together?'

'Because,' said the old lady firmly, 'enough is enough.'

⧼⧽

Horse or Chicken?

Prior to taking retirement and selling off his land, a farmer needed to get rid of all the animals he owned, so he decided to call on every house in his village. At houses where the man was the boss, he gave a horse; at houses where the woman was the boss, he gave a chicken.

Approaching one cottage, he saw a couple gardening and called out, 'Who's the boss around here?'

'I am,' said the man.

The farmer said: 'I have a black horse and a brown horse. Which one would you like?'

The man thought for a minute and said, 'The black one.'

'No, no, get the brown one,' said his wife.

The farmer said, 'Here's your chicken.'

A Slow Round

Two senior citizens went for a game of golf on a Sunday morning, but one of the men was under strict instructions from his wife to be home by one o'clock because friends were coming round for lunch.

One o'clock passed, as did two o'clock and three o'clock. Eventually, at four o'clock, the husband arrived home.

His wife was furious. 'You're three hours late,' she screamed. 'Where the hell have you been?' Our guests left half an hour ago.'

'I'm so sorry, darling,' he said, 'but a terrible thing happened on the golf course. We made it to the first green but then my playing partner, Jim, dropped dead from a heart attack.'

The wife started to feel guilty. 'Oh, that's awful,' she said.

'You're telling me,' said the husband. 'The rest of the round it was hit the ball, drag Jim, hit the ball, drag Jim . . .'

She's Trying to Poison Me

An elderly man went to the police station to report that he thought his wife was trying to poison him.

'Are you sure about this?' asked the officer.

'Absolutely,' replied the man. 'I am convinced that she's poisoning me slowly but surely. So what should I do?'

'Don't do anything just yet,' advised the officer, 'but remain vigilant at all times with regard to what you eat and drink. In the meantime I'll talk to your wife and attempt to ascertain whether or not your suspicions are justified. I'll get back to you.'

Ten days later, the police officer called the husband and said: 'Well, I've spoken to your wife. In fact, I talked to her on the phone for two and a half hours. Then she came down to the station and we talked for another four hours. Do you want my advice?'

'Yes,' said the husband anxiously.

'Take the poison.'

Going Downhill

An elderly lady visited the doctor with a list of complaints about her deteriorating health. Her joints were stiff, her back ached, her vision was on the decline and she had a weak bladder.
'I'm afraid,' said the doctor, 'you have to accept that as you get older things will start to go downhill. After all, who wants to live to a hundred?'
The woman replied, 'Anyone who's ninety-nine.'

Secret of a Long Life

The local pastor visited Maurice on his ninety-sixth birthday and asked him how he had managed to live to such a ripe old age.

'Well,' said Maurice, 'I believe it's because I have never touched a woman or a drop of drink in my whole life.'

The pastor nodded his head sagely. 'I do think there is a lot of truth in what you say.'

Just then there was a terrific crash and a scream from upstairs.

'What was that?' asked the pastor, startled.

'Oh, don't worry,' said Maurice. 'That was Dad. He's drunk again and is chasing the maid around the bedroom.'

Holiday Panic

A senior couple were relaxing on the beach on holiday when the wife suddenly yelled out: 'Oh my God! I've just remembered I left the oven on at home!'

'Don't worry,' said her husband reassuringly. 'The house won't burn down. I've just remembered I left the bath running!'

Morning Sickness

Three old men were talking about their aches, pains and bodily functions.

One complained,' I wake up every morning at seven and it takes me fifteen minutes to pee.'

'That's nothing.' said the second. 'I get up every morning at eight and it makes me half an hour of straining to produce a bowel movement. It's terrible.'

The third said, 'Every morning I pee like a horse at seven and crap like a cow at eight.'

'So what's your problem?' asked the others.

'I don't wake up till nine.'

Birthday Cake

To mark his wife's fiftieth birthday, a man placed an order by phone for a huge cake from the bakery. He said: 'The message I want is, ''You are not getting older, you are getting better''.'

The baker's assistant said: 'That's rather a lot of words. How do you want us to arrange them?'

After a moment's thought, the man said, 'Put ''You are not getting older'' at the top, ''You are getting better'' at the bottom.'

'Okay,' said the assistant, and he made a note of the

inscription to give to the baker.

Come the day of the birthday party, friends and family travelled from miles around to join in the celebrations. And then came the big moment: the unveiling of the cake.

To the wife's great embarrassment the words on the cake were clear to all: 'You are not getting older at the top, you are getting better at the bottom.'

A Good Catch

A rabbi was called to a Miami Beach nursing home to conduct a wedding. A nervous old man met him at the door. The rabbi sat him down and asked a serious of questions before deciding whether or not he would officiate.

'Do you love her?' asked the rabbi.

'I guess so,' replied the old man without any great enthusiasm.

'Is she a good Jewish woman?'

'I don't know for sure.'

'Does she have lots of money?' continued the rabbi.

'I doubt it.'

'Then why are you marrying her?'

'Because she can drive at night.'

Renewed Vows

A couple who had been married for forty-five years decided
they wanted to renew their vows. They discussed the details with
their grown-up children, and the wife described the dress she
was planning to wear.

'What colour shoes are you going to wear with it?' asked her
eldest daughter.

'I thought silver,' replied the wife.

'Yes,' laughed the husband, 'silver – to match her hair.'

At that, the wife glared at her husband's bald spot and shot
back: 'So I guess you're going barefoot?'

Not So Long

Two old men – Bert and Harry – were sitting quietly in a bar.
'When was the last time you made love to a woman?' Bert asked
Harry.

'1945,' replied Harry.

'My goodness!' exclaimed Bert. 'That's a long time ago.'

'Not really,' said Harry, glancing at his watch. 'It's only twenty
past eight now.'

Farmer's Warning

An official from the US Department of Highways stopped at a farm and talked to the elderly farmer. He told the farmer: 'I need to inspect your land with a view to building a new road.'

'Very well,' said the old farmer, 'but don't go in that field.'

The official replied loftily, 'I have the authority of the State of Texas to go wherever I want. See this card? I am allowed to go wherever I want on farm land.'

Seeing that there was no point in arguing with officialdom, the farmer went off and did some chores. A few minutes later, he heard loud screams and saw the official running from the field, hotly pursued by the farmer's prize bull.

The farmer called out: 'Show him your card, smartass!'

Breaking Bad News

Back in the 1950s, a wealthy middle-aged English businessman went on holiday to the Bahamas. While he was sunning himself, the hotel manager brought him a telegram from his butler. It read simply: 'CAT DEAD.' Distraught at the loss of his beloved pet, the businessman cut short his holiday and returned home. After giving the cat a decent burial in the garden, he remonstrated with his butler for the cold-hearted nature of the telegram.

'You should break bad news gently,' he said. 'If I had had to tell you that your cat had died, I would have sent a telegram saying: 'The cat's on the roof and can't get down.' Then a few hours later I would have sent another telegram saying: 'The cat's fallen off the roof and is badly hurt.' Finally a couple of hours after that I would have sent a third telegram saying: 'The cat has sadly passed away.' That way, you would have been gradually prepared for the bad news and would have been able to deal with it better.'

'I understand, sir,' said the butler. 'I will bear that in mind in future.'

The lecture over, the businessman booked another ticket to the Bahamas and resumed his holiday.

Two days later, he received another telegram from his butler: 'YOUR MOTHER ON ROOF CANNOT GET DOWN.'

The Worm That Turned

A small boy and his grandfather were raking leaves in the garden. The boy saw an earthworm trying to get back into its hole.

'Grandpa,' he cried, 'I bet I can put that worm back in that hole.'

'I'll bet you five pounds you can't,' said the grandfather. 'It's too wriggly and limp to put back in that little hole. You'll never get it in.'

The boy went into the house, came back with a can of hairspray and sprayed the worm until it was straight and stiff. Then he stuffed the worm back into the hole.

His grandpa gave him the five pounds and trotted indoors with a smile on his face. Forty-five minutes later, he reappeared and gave his grandson another five pounds.

'But, Grandpa, you already gave me five pounds.'

'I know. That's from your grandma.'

Sales Demonstration

A vacuum cleaner salesman knocked on the door of a house. It was answered by an elderly lady.

'Good morning, madam,' he began.

'Are you selling something?' she asked suspiciously.

'Well . . .'

'Because if it's insurance, double glazing or a new kitchen, I'm not interested!'

But before she could slam the door in his face, he blocked it with his foot and said: 'Madam, I promise you this will be worth your while. A demonstration of this amazing new vacuum cleaner will only take five minutes and will leave your carpet as good as new.'

'Oh, very well,' she said, and allowed him in.

Once inside, he emptied a bucket of horse manure onto her hallway carpet. 'If this vacuum cleaner does not remove every trace of this horse manure from your carpet, madam, I personally will eat the rest of it.'

The old lady said, 'Well, I hope you've got a healthy appetite, son, because they cut off my electricity this morning!'

A Lock of Hair

Two women neighbours met in the street. Eyeing the jewellery around her friend's neck, one said: 'What is in that locket? Is it a memento of some sort?'

'Yes,' replied the other woman. 'It's a lock of my husband's hair.'

'But your husband is still alive!'

'I know, but his hair's all gone.'

Lucky Women

Two old men were sitting in the park talking. After a while the conversation turned to ageing. One said, 'When it comes to getting older, women have all the luck.'

'How do you mean?' asked his friend.

'Well, I haven't been able to perform in bed for ten years now, but my wife seems to be healthier than ever.'

'In what way is she healthier?' asked the friend.

'Up to about ten years ago, she used to get these terrible headaches just before bedtime. But she doesn't get them any more.'

Diamond with a Curse

A man found himself seated next to an elegant, middle-aged woman on a plane. He couldn't help noticing that she was wearing the biggest diamond ring he had ever seen.

'I was just admiring your diamond ring,' he said by way of conversation.

'This is the Rosenbloom diamond,' she said. 'It is very beautiful, but there is a terrible curse that goes with it.'

'Oh, really?' said the man. 'What's the curse?

The woman replied, 'Mr Rosenbloom.'

Kitchen Confusion

An elderly man asked his wife to prepare him a chocolate ice cream sundae. She went to the kitchen and returned half an hour later with a plate of scrambled eggs.

Seeing this, he complained, 'Where are the sausages? I asked for sausages!'

Marriage Counselling

A couple who had been married for forty years were entertaining friends at a dinner party when the conversation turned to marriage counselling.

'We'll never need that,' said the wife confidently. 'George and I have a great relationship. You see, it's all a question of education.'

'How do you mean?' asked one of the friends.

'Well, she continued, 'at college, George did a communications course and I studied drama. So he communicates really well and I act like I'm listening.'

A Voice from the Grave

A known hypochondriac, Mrs Jones regularly visited her doctor to complain about various imaginary illnesses. He always palmed her off with a mild sedative, which kept her happy for a couple of weeks.

One day she came in to his surgery complaining of chest pains. He prescribed the usual sedative but this time her pain was genuine and the following day she died of a heart attack. The doctor was so distraught by his error that he immediately dropped dead from shock.

Later that week, Mrs Jones and the doctor were buried in adjacent plots at the local cemetery. The morning after the funerals, the doctor heard a tapping sound on his coffin. A muffled voice called out: 'Doctor, this is Mrs Jones. Do you have anything for worms?'

Don't Make Assumptions

An eighty-year-old man went to the doctor for a check-up. After giving him a thorough medical, the doctor declared: 'You're in great shape. At this rate, you might live for ever! Tell me, how old was your father when he died?'

'Did I say he was dead?' said the old man.

The doctor was amazed. 'Well, how old was your grandfather when he died?'

'Did I say he was dead?'

'This is unbelievable!' exclaimed the doctor. 'You mean to say, you're eighty years old, and both your father and grandfather are still alive?'

'Not only that,' said the old man proudly, 'but my grandfather, who is now 122, has just got married for the first time.'

The doctor was almost speechless. 'After 122 years of living as a bachelor, what on earth would make your grandfather want to get married?'

'Did I say he wanted to?'

Hearing Voices

An elderly patient went to the doctor. 'I need your help, doctor,' he said. 'Do you remember those voices in my head which I've been complaining about for years?'

'Yes.'

'Well, they've suddenly stopped.'

'That's good. So what's the problem?'

'I think I might be going deaf.'

Note to the Taxman

A dying man, who had no surviving family members, summoned his accountant to his deathbed. He said, 'When I die, I want you to have my remains cremated.'

'And what would you like me to do with your ashes?' asked the accountant.

The old man replied, 'Put them in an envelope and mail them to the Inland Revenue with a note saying, "Now you have everything."'

Large Family

A couple had been married for forty-six years, during which time they had raised eleven children and been blessed with twenty-six grandchildren. When asked the secret of how they had managed to stay together for so long, they said, 'Years ago we made a promise to each other: the first one to pack up and leave had to take all the kids.'

Light Sleeper

When an elderly couple woke up one morning, the husband asked: 'Did you hear that terrible storm last night?'

'No,' said the wife. 'Was there thunder?'

'Yes, it was awful. It sounded like the end of the world.'

'Why didn't you wake me?' she said tetchily. 'You know I can never sleep when it thunders.'

A Tap on the Shoulder

To top up his pension, a retired man took a part-time job as a taxi driver. On his first day, he was driving along when his passenger suddenly tapped him on the shoulder. The taxi driver immediately screamed, lost control of the cab and swerved violently across the road, nearly smashing into a wall.

As he sat there gasping for breath, he said to the passenger: 'Don't ever do that to me again. You scared the hell out of me.'

'I'm sorry,' said the passenger. 'I didn't realize that a tap on the shoulder could be so terrifying.'

'It's not really your fault,' said the driver. 'It's just that today is my first day driving a cab. For the past thirty-nine years I've been driving a hearse.'

Viagra Request

A ninety-one-year-old man went into a pharmacy and asked for Viagra tablets, which he wanted cut into quarters.

The pharmacist said, 'Sure I can do that for you, but you do realize that a quarter of a tablet won't give you a full erection?'

The old man replied: 'I'm ninety-one. I'm too old for that game. I just want it to stick out far enough so that I don't pee on my slippers.'

Patient Update

A senior man telephoned his local hospital and asked: 'How is Mr Ratcliffe in Ward 35?'

The duty nurse replied, 'Mr Ratcliffe is progressing well. His test results were fine and the doctors are very pleased with him. Can I ask who is calling?'

'Yes, this is Mr Ratcliffe in Ward 35,' said the caller. 'No one tells me anything.'

Almost Every Night

A seventy-six-year-old man married a woman less than half his age and took her off on honeymoon to the Caribbean. When he returned home, his sister asked him how it had gone.

'Oh, it was wonderful,' he said. 'We made love almost every night.'

'That's quite a feat at your age,' said the sister.

'Yes,' he continued. 'Almost Monday, almost Tuesday, almost Wednesday . . .'

Marriage Vows

An elderly couple were having their first major row after thirty-six years of marriage.

'When we got married, you promised to love, honour and obey,' the wife said:

'I know,' said the husband, 'but I didn't want to start an argument in front of all those people.'

Spare Keys

A senior couple were arguing about the wife's practice of leaving her car keys in the ignition.

'But if I take them out of the ignition, I can never find them again,' she explained.

'That's all very well,' the husband said, 'but what happens if someone steals the car?'

'No problem,' the wife insisted. 'I keep a spare set of keys in the glove compartment.'

The Golfing Assistant

'How was your golf game, dear?' asked Jim's wife Helen.

'I hit the ball pretty well, but my eyesight has got so bad that I could never see where it went.'

'Face facts,' said Helen. 'You're seventy-two now. Why don't you take my brother Jack along?'

'But Jack's eighty-one and doesn't even play any more.'

'I know, but he's got perfect eyesight and could watch your ball for you.'

So Jim agreed to take Jack along to his next game. At the first hole, Jim sent his drive sailing into the distance. 'Did you see where it went?' he asked Jack.

'Sure did,' said Jack.

'Well, where is it?' said Jim as they set off in pursuit.

'I forget.'

I Know You . . .

In the States, a small-town prosecuting attorney called his first witness to the stand in a trial – an elderly grandmother. He approached her and asked her, 'Mrs Johnson, do you know me?'

'I certainly do know you, Mr Fletcher,' she replied. 'I've known you since you were a young boy – and frankly you've been a big disappointment to me. You lie, you cheat on your wife, you manipulate people and you talk about them behind their backs. You think you're a rising big shot when you haven't the brains to realize you'll never amount to anything more than a two-bit paper pusher. Yes, I know you.'

The lawyer was stunned. Not knowing what else to do, he pointed across the room and asked, 'Mrs Johnson, do you know the defence attorney?'

'Yes, I do,' she answered. 'I've also known Mr Kelly since he was a youngster. I used to baby-sit him for his parents – and he, too, has been a big disappointment to me. He's lazy, he's bigoted, and he's got a real drinking problem. The man can't build a normal relationship with anyone and his law practice is generally considered to be one of the shoddiest in the entire state. Yes, I know him.'

At that point the judge rapped the courtroom to silence and called both counsellors to the bench. In a very quiet voice, he said menacingly, 'If either of you asks her if she knows me, you'll go straight to jail for contempt!'

Always There

After thirty-three years of marriage, a husband stunned his wife by telling her that he wanted a divorce.

'But, Colin,' she pleaded, 'how could you want to divorce me after everything we've been through together? Do you remember how shortly after we met, you caught that terrible virus and nearly died, but I helped you pull through? And when you were attacked by a shark on that surfing holiday in South Africa, I summoned the ambulance to rush you to hospital. Then when your family were wiped out in that tragic fire, I comforted you. And when you were falsely accused of fraud, I put up the bail money and stood by you. Even when you lost all that money on property development, I was there for you. How could you leave me? We've been through so much.'

'That's the problem, Joan,' he said. 'All these years, you've brought me nothing but bad luck!'

Looking Forward

Three elderly gentlemen were talking about what their grandchildren would be saying about them in fifty years' time.

The first said, 'I would like my grandchildren to say, "He was great fun to be with."'

'Fifty years from now,' said the second, 'I want mine to say, "He was a loyal and loving family man."'

Turning to the third man, they asked him, 'So what do you want them to say about you in fifty years?'

'I want them to say,' the third man replied, '"He looks really good for his age!"'

I'm a Senior Citizen . . .

I'm very good at telling stories . . . over and over and over.

I'm the life and soul of the party – even when it lasts as late as 8 p.m.

I'm the first one to find the bathroom wherever I go.

I'm awake at least three hours before my body allows me to get up.

I'm usually interested in getting home before I get to where I'm going.

I'm anti-everything: anti-smoking, anti-noise, anti-inflammatory.

I'm wrinkled, saggy and lumpy – and that's just my left leg.

I'm able to keep in touch with friends through the obituary column.

I'm smiling all the time because I can't hear a word you're saying.

I'm a walking storeroom of facts; I've just lost the key.

Virgin Death

An elderly lady was proud of being a virgin. Before she passed away, she issued strict instructions to the funeral director regarding her headstone. 'I want it to read: "Born as a virgin, lived as a virgin, died as a virgin."' When she died, the funeral director relayed the orders to the men inscribing her headstone. But they were lazy, and instead of carving out the full inscription, they just wrote, 'Returned unopened.'

The Last Night

A man in his sixties returned from the doctor and revealed to his wife that he was terminally ill and had only twenty hours to live. In view of the grim prognosis, he asked his wife for sex, and she readily agreed and they made love.

Six hours later, he said to her, 'Honey, you know I have only fourteen hours to live. Could we please have sex one last time?'

The wife agreed, and they made love again.

That evening as the man climbed into bed, he looked at his watch and realized he had only eight hours to live. So he tapped his wife on the shoulder and said: 'Please, honey, one more time before I die.'

She said, 'Okay, darling,' and they made love for a third time.

Four hours later, he woke her from a deep sleep. 'Honey,' he said. 'I only have four hours to live. How about we have sex one last time?'

'Listen,' she snapped, 'I have to get up in the morning – you don't!'

Lost Wives

Two men – one old, one young – were pushing their trolleys around the supermarket when they collided. 'Oh, I'm so sorry,' they both said.

'I was looking for my wife, and I guess I wasn't paying attention to where I was going,' The old man explained.

'That's a coincidence,' said the young man. 'I'm looking for my wife, too. I can't think where she's got to, but I know she's around here somewhere.'

'Well maybe we can help each other,' said the old man. 'What does your wife look like?'

'She's twenty-six with long blonde hair, long slim legs, blue eyes,' the young man replied, 'and she's wearing a short skirt, tight-fitting black top and knee-length boots. What does your wife look like?'

'Never mind,' said the old man eagerly. 'Let's look for yours first.'

Guilt Trip

A young man felt guilty about not having spoken to his widowed mother for over a month, so he decided to give her a call.

'How are you?' he asked.

'Not so good,' she answered sadly. 'I have been feeling very weak.'

'Why have you been weak?' he asked, concerned.

'Because I haven't eaten in thirty-six days.'

'How come you haven't eaten in thirty-six days?'

'Because,' she replied, 'I didn't want my mouth to be full of food when you called.'

Night Call

A librarian was fast asleep in bed at three o'clock in the morning when his home phone rang. He answered it, and an elderly lady's voice on the other end of the line said: 'What time does the library open?'

'Nine o'clock,' replied the librarian wearily. 'And what do you mean by calling me at home in the middle of the night to ask me such a thing?'

'Not until nine o'clock?' said the old lady dejectedly.

'No, not until nine o'clock,' snapped the librarian. 'Why do you want to get in before nine o'clock?'

'I don't want to get in,' said the old lady. 'I want to get out!'

Change of Plan

An attractive young girl, chaperoned by an ugly old crone, entered the doctor's office. 'We have come for an examination,' said the young girl.

'Right,' said the doctor. 'Go behind that curtain and take your clothes off.'

'No, it's not for me,' said the girl. 'It's for my elderly aunt here.'

'Very well . . . Madam, put your tongue out.'

Small Consolation

The doctor said to his elderly patient, 'I have some good news and some bad news. The bad news is that we have had to amputate both your legs.'

'What's the good news?' asked the patient, horrified.

'The man in the next bed wants to buy your slippers.'

Secrets of the Trade

A couple in their sixties went to see a stage show featuring an illusionist. They were so impressed by his act that afterwards they went backstage to meet him.

'Tell me,' said the husband, 'how did you do that stunt with the swords? It was absolutely incredible.'

'I could tell you,' smiled the illusionist, 'but then I'd have to kill you!'

'Okay,' said the husband. 'Just tell my wife.'

Were You Ever Unfaithful?

As they celebrated their fiftieth wedding anniversary, a husband asked his wife, 'Tell me honestly, have you ever cheated on me?'

'That's a funny question to ask after all these years,' she said, surprised. 'But if you really want to know, yes, I have cheated on you – on three occasions.'

The husband was saddened by the confession but wanted to know the exact details.

'The first time was when you were in your late twenties,' said his wife. 'Remember you wanted to start a business but no bank would give you a loan? And remember how the bank president came to our house in person and signed the documents? Well . . .'

The husband was touched. 'You mean you slept with the president of the bank just so that I could start up my own business? That's the sweetest thing anybody has ever done for me. When was the second occasion?'

'Remember when you were forty you had a heart attack and no surgeon would operate on you? And then Dr Dreyfuss came all the way up here to perform the surgery himself? Well . . .'

The husband was genuinely moved. 'So you mean to say that you slept with Dr Dreyfuss to save my life? What an amazing woman you are! I'm so lucky to have you as my wife. So tell me, when was the third occasion?'

'Remember how a few years ago you really wanted to be president of the golf club? But you were fifty-seven votes short . . . ?'

The Talkative Wife

A police officer pulled over a speeding car. The officer told the middle-aged driver: 'I clocked you at over eighty miles an hour, sir.'

'I don't understand it, officer,' said the driver. ' I had the car on cruise control at sixty. Perhaps your radar gun is faulty.'

Without looking up from her knitting, the driver's wife in the passenger seat said, 'Don't be silly, dear. You know this car doesn't have cruise control.'

As the officer started to write out a ticket, the driver turned to his wife and growled, 'Can't you keep your mouth shut for once?'

The wife smiled sweetly and replied, 'You should be grateful your radar detector went off when it did.'

As the officer made out a second ticket for possessing an illegal radar detector unit, the driver glowered at his wife and said through clenched teeth, 'Damn it, woman, can't you ever keep your mouth shut?'

The officer frowned. 'And I notice that you're not wearing your seat belt, sir. That's an automatic £30 fine,' he said.

The driver explained: 'Well, you see, officer, I had it on but I took it off when you pulled me over so that I could get my licence out of my back pocket.'

The wife interrupted: 'Now, dear, you know very well that you didn't have your seat belt on. You never wear it when you're driving.'

As the officer wrote out a third ticket for seat belt violation, the driver turned to his wife and yelled: 'For the last time, woman, shut up!'

The police officer looked over to the wife. 'Does your husband always talk to you like this?' he asked.

'No, officer,' she replied. 'Only when he's been drinking.'

Mixed Blessing

After years of suffering from impaired hearing, a man was finally given a new hearing aid that allowed him to hear perfectly. Monitoring his patient's progress, the doctor remarked, 'I'm sure your family are delighted that at last you can hear again.'

The man said: 'I haven't told them yet. I just sit around and listen to their conversations. I've changed my will five times in the last two months!'

Cruel Trick

At a large family gathering, a group of mischievous teenagers decided to see what would happen if they put a Viagra tablet in their grandfather's drink. After a while, Grandad had to excuse himself and go to the gents'. When he returned, the front of his trousers was wet all over.

'What happened?' asked his concerned children.

'Well,' said Grandad, 'I had to go to the loo. So I took it out, but then I saw that it wasn't mine, so I put it back again.'

Fatal Attraction

An old man announced that he was planning to marry a young actress on his seventy-seventh birthday.

'Do be careful,' his doctor warned him. 'Prolonged sex with a girl that young could be fatal.'

The old man shrugged. 'If she dies, she dies.'

Blame Grandma

Having missed a film they wanted to see at the cinema, a middle-aged couple eagerly accepted the invitation of their friends to go and watch it at their house one evening when it came out on DVD. Since the husband's ninety-year-old mother lived with them and they were worried about leaving her alone, they asked whether she could come too. The friends said yes.

So they all settled down to watch the film but after about half an hour, the husband, feeling the effects of a hard day at work, started to nod off. He startled himself awake a few times but eventually he turned to his wife and said he thought they should be going home because mother was probably tired.

The old lady was indignant. 'It's you who's tired,' she said. 'Not me.' Then turning to the hosts, she added, 'Next time you invite me, I'll be sure to leave the children at home!'

A Reformed Alcoholic

An old man with a red nose went into a hardware store and said, 'I'll have a bottle of meths, please.'

The shop assistant looked at him suspiciously and said: 'There's no way I'm selling you a bottle of methylated spirit – you'll drink it.'

'No I won't,' the old man protested. 'I'm starting my own painting and decorating business.'

'I don't believe you,' said the assistant, 'because I know who you are; you're the old drunk who sits on the bench in the park.'

'I used to be,' admitted the old man, 'but I've turned my life around. The trouble is people like you won't let me forget. I'll always be that drunkard no matter how hard I work, and that's what hurts so much.'

The assistant was overcome with guilt. 'Okay,' he said, 'I'm sorry. Here's your bottle of meths.'

'You haven't got a cold one, have you?' the old man asked.

Art Critic

A little old lady was attending an exhibition at an art gallery. She studied one abstract painting at length and simply couldn't make out what it was supposed to be. Finally she asked the artist, who was standing nearby, 'What on earth is that?'

'That, my dear lady,' he said condescendingly, 'is meant to be a mother and her child.'

'Well then,' snapped the little old lady, 'why isn't it?'

The Refund

An elderly man approached a church minister and said, 'Excuse me, but do you think a man ought to profit from the mistakes of others?'

The churchman considered the question carefully before

answering: 'No, I don't think he should.'

'In that case,' said the man, 'I would like my twenty pounds back.'

'Twenty pounds?' queried the minister. 'What do you mean?'

The man said: 'That's what you charged for my wedding ceremony back in 1968.'

Neighbourly Concern

Worried that they hadn't heard or seen the widow in the neighbouring apartment for three days, a mother said to her young son, 'Will you go next door and see how old Mrs Champion is?'

A few minutes later, the boy returned.

'Is she all right?' asked the mother.

'Yes, she's fine,' said the boy. 'Except that she's angry at you.'

'Angry at me? Whatever for?'

'She said it's none of your business how old she is.'

Suicide Bid

Distraught at being left a widow at the age of ninety-four, Edith decided to commit suicide so that she could join her husband in heaven. In an attempt to ensure that her death was as swift and painless as possible, she rang her doctor to ask precisely where the human heart is located.

'It's just below the left breast,' he told her.

Acting on this information, she took her husband's gun, placed it in the correct spot, and fired. Twenty minutes later she was admitted to hospital with a gunshot wound – to her left knee.

Changing a Light Bulb

An elderly man with one arm bumped into an old friend.
'Where are you off to?' asked the friend.
'To change a light bulb,' replied the one-armed man.
'That will be a bit difficult for you, won't it?'
'No, not really,' said the one-armed man. 'I kept the receipt.'

Off His Rocker

An old timer was beginning to feel his age. 'Your gout is getting worse,' his doctor told him. 'I recommend that you give up smoking, drinking and sex for a while.'

'What!' exclaimed the old man. 'Just so I can walk a little better? If it wasn't for smoking, drinking and sex, I wouldn't get out of my rocker in the first place!'

Playing Safe

An old man stood up slowly and put on his coat.

'Where are you going?' asked his equally aged wife.

'I'm going to the doctor's,' he replied.

'Why? Are you sick?'

'No,' he said, 'I'm going to get some of those Viagra pills that everyone keeps going on about.'

Hearing this, the wife climbed from her rocker and put on her coat.

'Where are you going?' he demanded.

'I'm going to the doctor's, too,' she said, 'because if you're going to start using that rusty old thing, I'm going to get a tetanus shot!'

Top of the Range

A man was excitedly telling his friend about his new hearing aid. 'It's the best on the market,' he enthused. 'It wasn't cheap, but, believe me, it was worth every penny.'

'What kind is it?' asked the friend.

'Half past three.'

A Persistent Cough

An elderly man with a persistent cough went to the pharmacist in search of a cure for his ailment. The assistant recommended a standard cough remedy but a week later the man was back complaining that the cure was not working. So the assistant gave him a different cough medicine but once again the man returned a week later to say that this was not working either. This time he saw the head pharmacist.

A week later, the head pharmacist and his assistant looked out of the window and saw the man walking very slowly down the street. He didn't cough once..

'That's amazing,' said the assistant. 'What cough remedy did you give him?'

'I didn't give him a cough remedy,' replied the pharmacist. 'I gave him a laxative. Now he's afraid to cough.'

Exercise Bike

Two senior ladies met for coffee and began discussing their respective husbands. As the conversation turned to health matters, one asked: 'Can your Charlie still perform in bed?'

'He makes me feel like an exercise bike,' said the other.

'How's that?'

'He climbs on and starts pumping away but we never get anywhere.'

The Old Feller

An old man went for an interview with a logging company for a job as a tree feller. The boss of the company took one look at the old man's frail body and thought he would be scarcely capable of even lifting an axe but since the old man had travelled over thirty miles for the interview, the boss decided to give him a chance to show what he could do.

So the old man was led into the woods where he was told to chop down a pine tree that measured more than three feet in diameter. The old man promptly wielded his trusty axe and felled the tree with a single blow. The boss could hardly believe his eyes. Next the old man was told to fell a row of giant fir trees, each with trunks over four feet thick. A few blows from the axe and the trees were brought to the ground.

The boss scratched his head in disbelief. 'Where did you learn to fell trees like that?' he asked.

'In the Sahara Forest,' replied the old man.

'You mean the Sahara Desert?' said the owner, correcting him.

'Well, yes,' said the old man, leaning casually on his axe, 'that's what they call it now.'

Retirement Card

Finally at an age when he had to retire from his own company, a boss decided to mark the occasion with a farewell party. He wanted all of his staff to express their appreciation for him on a card, which was duly sent round to each department for signature. But when the card was returned, he was disappointed to read stock phrases like 'The place won't be the same without you' and 'Wishing you a happy retirement.'

So he said to one of his longest-serving employees, 'John, you've been with me for twenty years. I want your comment on my card to be from the heart, to express how you really feel about my retirement after working with me for so long.'

Slowly but firmly, John wrote on the card: 'The best news in twenty years.'

Three Pills

An elderly man went to the doctor and said that he hadn't been feeling too well. After examining him thoroughly, the doctor produced three different types of pill.

'Take the green pill with a big glass of water first thing in the morning; take the blue pill with a big glass of water after lunch; and take the red pill with a big glass of water just before you go to bed at night,' He told his patient.

Startled to be on so much medicine, the old man stammered, 'What exactly is wrong with me, doctor?'

'You're not drinking enough water.'

Be Careful What You Wish For

A married couple in their early sixties were celebrating their thirty-fifth wedding anniversary in a quiet, romantic restaurant. Suddenly a small fairy appeared on their table and declared, 'As a reward for being such a devoted married couple who have been faithful and loving to each other for thirty-five years, I will grant you each a wish.'

The wife said: 'My wish is to be able to travel around the world with my dear husband.'

The fairy waved her magic wand and – *poof!* – two tickets for a luxury cruise liner appeared before their very eyes.

The husband thought for a moment. 'That's all very romantic but this is a chance in a lifetime, so I'm sorry, darling, but my wish is to have a wife who is thirty years younger than me.'

The fairy waved her magic wand and – *poof!* – the husband became ninety-three.

Zip Trouble

An elderly man went to his doctor and said: 'Doctor, I think I'm getting senile. Several times lately, I have forgotten to zip up.'

'That's not senility,' replied the doctor. 'Senility is when you forget to zip down.'

In Loving Memory

An old lady's two cats died within a few weeks of each other. Finding the house empty without them, she decided to take their bodies to a taxidermist so that they could be put on display in her living-room.

'These are my two cats,' she told the taxidermist. 'They used to be such good friends.'

'That's nice,' said the taxidermist. 'Tell me, do you want them stuffed and mounted?'

'No,' replied the old lady. 'Just holding hands.'

White Hair

A little girl was helping to unload the shopping when she noticed for the first time that her mother had a few white strands standing out from her brunette head. Inquisitive, she asked her mother, 'Why are some of your hairs white?'

The mother smiled. 'Every time you do something naughty or make me unhappy, one of my hairs turns white.'

The little girl thought about this for a moment .'So is that why *all* of Grandma's hairs are white?' she asked.

Are We There Yet?

A little old lady was on a Greyhound bus travelling south out of Quebec. After just a few minutes of the journey, she walked up to the front of the coach. 'Are we at Montreal yet?' she asked the driver.

'No,' said the driver. 'Don't worry, I'll let you know when we are.'

Fifteen minutes later, she asked him again, 'Are we at Montreal yet?'

'No,' he answered, struggling to remain polite. 'Like I say, I'll let you know when we are.'

She kept this up for the next four hours. Every fifteen minutes or so, she would totter down to the front of the coach and ask the driver whether they were at Montreal yet, and each time he would tell her firmly, 'No.' Finally, with his nerves ripped to shreds, Montreal bus station came into view and the relieved driver announced, 'Right, madam, this is Montreal. Off you get.'

'Oh no, driver,' she said. 'I'm going all the way to Toronto. It's just that my son told me that when I got to Montreal I should take my blood pressure tablet.'

A Private Wager

Now in their eighties, Tom and Harry had been friends since school. Even at their advanced age, they enjoyed nothing more than playing jokes on each other and making silly bets.

One day Tom said to Harry, 'I bet you a thousand dollars that mine is longer soft than yours is hard.'

'If you know anything about human anatomy, you'll know that's impossible,' said Harry.

'I want a bet, not a lecture' interrupted Tom. 'Mine is longer soft than yours is hard. A thousand dollars. Yes or no?'

'Okay, okay,' said Harry. 'I'll take the bet. How long is yours soft?'

Tom answered, 'Eleven years!'

Road Rage

A lady in her sixties was waiting patiently to drive into a parking space when a flash young city banker nipped in ahead of her in his brand-new Porsche. She was so upset by his rudeness that she went over to berate him.

'That was my parking space, young man!' she cried.

'Tough luck!' he sneered. 'You see, that's what you can do when you're young and smart!'

The lady was understandably incensed by his attitude. So she climbed back into her car, put her foot down hard and deliberately drove straight into the rear end of his Porsche, inflicting wholesale damage.

'What do you think you're doing, you stupid old woman?' he yelled. 'Are you crazy?'

She smiled and replied calmly, 'You see, that's what you can do when you're old and rich!'

The Secret

A couple celebrating their golden wedding anniversary were known among their friends for having the happiest marriage in town. Throughout their fifty years together, nobody had ever seen them exchange a cross word. To mark their anniversary, the local newspaper sent a reporter to interview them, and he asked them the secret of their domestic bliss.

'Well,' explained the husband, 'it all dates back to the honeymoon we took in Mexico. We were travelling by mule, and we hadn't gone far when my wife's mule stumbled. My wife said quietly, "That's once." We carried on a few hundred yards more and then the mule stumbled again. My wife said quietly, "That's twice." Half a mile further on, the mule stumbled for a third time. My wife promptly jumped down off the mule's back, pulled out a revolver and shot it dead.

'I immediately started to protest over her treatment of the mule, but she simply looked at me and said quietly, "That's once."'

Wedding Planner

After courting for over fifty years, a couple finally decided to get married. While out planning for the wedding, they called in at a drugstore.

The man asked the sales assistant, 'Do you sell pills for arthritis?'

'Yes, we do,' replied the assistant.

'Have you got anything to relieve constipation?'

'Yes, we have.'

'How about heart medication?'

'Yes, sir, we stock a wide range of tablets.'

'Sleeping pills?'

'Yes.'

'Denture cleaner?'

'Of course.'

'Right then!' said the man, nodding to his bride-to-be. 'We'd like to register here for our wedding gifts.'

Mixed Blessings

An elderly man went to the doctor for his test results. The doctor said, 'I've got good news and bad news.'

'What's the bad news?' asked the man.

The doctor replied, 'I'm afraid you've only got a week to live.'

'Oh my God!' exclaimed the old man. 'That's terrible! So what's the good news?'

The doctor said, 'They're going to name the disease after you.'

Wild Thing

Told that he had just twenty-four hours to live, a man in his fifties decided to go home and make passionate love to his wife. He crept into the bedroom, slid into bed and for the next three hours enjoyed the wildest sex he had ever experienced. Finally exhausted, he crawled into the bathroom where he was surprised to find his wife lying in the bath with a mudpack on her face.

'How did you get in here?' he asked.

'Ssssh!' she said. 'You'll wake my mother.'

Worst Cook in the World

After being married for over forty years to the worst cook in the world, a man arrived home from work one evening to find her in floods of tears.

'What's the matter, darling?' he asked.

'It's a disaster,' she wailed. 'The cat's eaten your dinner!'

'Don't worry,' said the husband, comforting her. 'I'll get you a new cat.'

Taking Precautions

At his annual check-up, an elderly man was asked by his doctor about his sex life.

'It's never been so good,' the old man enthused. 'Only last week, I picked up no fewer than four beautiful young girls – not one of them a day over thirty.'

'My goodness!' exclaimed the doctor. 'Well, I hope you took precautions.'

'Of course I did,' said the old man. 'I gave them all a false name.'

Will It Help My Golf?

A middle-aged man was prescribed a course of tablets for two months. He asked the doctor, 'Will I be able to play golf?'

'Yes, definitely,' said the doctor.

'That's great,' said the man, 'because I never could before!'

An Act of Jealousy

A wife arrived home from her weekly shopping trip to find her ninety-six-year-old husband in bed with another woman. In a jealous rage, she pushed him off the balcony of their apartment and sent him tumbling to his death. She was charged with murder and at her trial the judge asked her whether there was anything she wanted to say by way of mitigation.

'Well, your honour,' she said coolly, 'I figured that at ninety-six, if he could make love to another woman, he could fly, too!'

A Lift Home

On patrol in their car one night, two police officers spotted a drunken old lady staggering down the street. Instead of putting her in the cells for the night, they decided to drive her home.

One of the officers sat in the back of the car with her and as they drove through the streets, he asked her where she lived. She stroked him on the arm and answered, 'You're passionate.'

They drove on a little further and then the officer again asked her where she lived. Once more, she touched his arm and replied, 'You're passionate.'

Ten minutes later, the officer decided to see whether she had sobered up sufficiently to give a sensible reply.

'Where do you live?' he asked.

Again she caressed his arm and said, 'You're passionate.'

Fed up with this behaviour, the officer said, 'Look, madam, we've been driving around this city for over forty-five minutes and you still won't tell us where you live.'

The old woman replied, 'I keep trying to tell you: You're passin' it!'

The Visitor

A middle-aged couple were entertaining an old friend whom they hadn't been in touch with since school. 'Shortly after we were married,' began the husband, recapping their life story, 'we were blessed with a lovely, chubby creature with cute bow legs and no teeth.'

'Oh, how wonderful!' exclaimed the friend. 'You had a baby!'

'No,' said the husband. 'Jean's mother came to live with us!'

Signs That You're Not As Young As You Used To Be

* Suddenly middle-aged people are not forty-five, they're *only* forty-five.

* Before throwing the local paper away, you look through the property section.
* If you do go to a club, you leave before the end to beat the rush.
* You always have enough milk in.
* You sink your teeth into a steak and they stay there.
* Before going out anywhere, you ask if there is a place to park.
* Pop music all starts to sound the same.
* Whenever you fall asleep, people worry that you're dead.
* You don't buy green bananas.
* You have more hair in your ears than on your head.
* A night on the tiles means a long game of Scrabble.
* You're still chasing women, but you can't remember why.
* You start doing jigsaw puzzles again.
* Your wife gives up sex for Lent and you don't find out until Easter.
* When sitting outside a pub you start to admire their hanging baskets.
* You have a party and the neighbours don't even realize it.
* Your back goes out more than you do.
* You buy T-shirts without anything written on them.
* The glint in your eyes is from the sun hitting your bifocals.
* You find yourself saying, 'Is it cold in here or is it just me?'

Find Another Husband

On his deathbed, a husband gasped weakly to his wife: 'Please, my dear, I want you to grant me one last wish.'

'What is it?' she asked.

'Six months after I die I want you to marry Ken from next door.'

'But I thought you hated Ken,' she said.

'I do,' said the husband.

Parking Spot

After enduring forty-two years of a miserable marriage, a husband did not shed too many tears when his wife finally passed away. He refused to spend much money on her funeral and to save on burial costs he arranged for her to be buried privately in their back garden.

A week later, the dead wife's brother called at the house to pay his respects and was surprised to see her bottom protruding from the soil.

'Did you bury her like that as a mark of affection,' asked the brother, 'so that you could always see her and feel in touch with her?'

'Certainly not,' snapped the husband. 'It's somewhere to park my bike!'

Genteel Home

Two middle-aged brothers and their middle-aged sister brought their frail, elderly mother to a nursing home, where, having settled her down, they left her, hoping she would be well cared for. The next morning, the nurses bathed her, gave her a good breakfast, and settled her in an armchair next to a window overlooking a lovely garden. She smiled and seemed happy, but after a while she started to lean slowly over sideways in her chair.

Two attentive nurses immediately rushed up to catch her and straightened her up.

She seemed fine, but after a while she started to tilt to the other side. The nurses rushed back and once more brought her back upright. This went on all morning.

In the afternoon, her family arrived to see how she was settling into her new home.

'So, Ma, how is it here? Are they treating you all right?' they asked.

'It's quite nice,' she replied. 'Except they won't let you fart.'

The Best Thing
A newspaper reporter was interviewing a 104-year-old woman. 'What's the best thing about being 104?' he asked her.
'No peer pressure,' she replied.

Not Much of a Compliment

A woman was standing naked in front of the mirror. 'Look at me,' she said sadly to her husband, 'I'm old and fat. Cheer me up by paying me a compliment.'

The husband said: 'Your eyesight is still good.'

The Wedding Dress

A young woman who was getting married asked whether she could wear her mother's wedding dress on the big day. Seeing her daughter walk into the room for the first time, the gown a perfect fit on her petite frame, made the mother burst into tears.

The daughter gave her a comforting hug. 'Don't cry,' she said. 'Remember you mustn't think of it as losing a daughter, you must think of it as gaining a son.'

'That's not why I'm crying,' sobbed the mother. 'I used to fit into that dress!'

Where's the Baby?

Having undergone fertility treatment, a woman was able to give birth at the age of sixty-six. When she was discharged from hospital, her relatives came to visit.

'Can we see the baby?' they asked.

'Not yet,' replied the sixty-six-year-old mother.

Fifteen minutes later, they asked again, 'Can we see the baby?'

'Not yet,' she said.

Another fifteen minutes passed and they asked again, 'Can we see the baby?'

'Not yet,' said the mother.

By now the relatives were getting impatient. 'Well, *when* can we see the baby?'

'When it cries.'

'Why do we have to wait until the baby cries?'

'Because I've forgotten where I put it.'

A Cunning Plan

From his home in Florida, Jack phoned his son in New York and announced, 'Michael, I'm going to divorce your mother.'

'You can't,' said a shocked Michael. 'You two have been married for forty-four years.'

'I'm sorry,' said Jack, 'but I don't want to discuss it. My mind is made up. I just thought I ought to let you know.'

'Can I talk to Mom?' asked Michael.

'No, I don't want you talking to her for the simple reason that I haven't told her yet. But I'm seeing a lawyer the day after tomorrow.'

Michael couldn't believe his ears. 'Listen, Dad, don't do anything rash. You can't throw your whole life away just like that. I'll catch the first flight down, and we can talk about it rationally as a family before you start seeing lawyers. Does that sound fair?'

'Very well,' sighed Jack. 'I'll postpone the lawyer for a day or two. Will you call your sister and break the news to her? I can't bear to talk about it any more.'

Less than an hour later, Jack received a phone call from his daughter in New Jersey. She said that she and her brother had already bought tickets online and that they and the children would be arriving in Florida the following evening. She made him promise not to do anything hasty.

Jack promised, and put down the phone. Then he turned to his wife and said, 'Darling, it worked! . . . But I wonder what we can do to get them to come down next year?'

Forgetful Spouse

A wife in her fifties went to see a lawyer and told him: 'I want to divorce my husband.'

'On what grounds?' asked the lawyer.

'Because he has a lousy memory,' replied the wife.

'How is that a reason for divorce?'

The wife said icily, 'Whenever he sees a young woman, he forgets that he's married.'

Weight of Years

Bill, who is due to retire from the building trade in a few months, is often the butt of his colleagues' jokes, and is getting fed up with them always taunting him about his age and failing strength (and failing other things too). He turns to Liam, the youngest of the builders, always showing off his muscles, and says, 'See that wheelbarrow there? I bet I can push it over to that wall carrying a load that you won't be able to push back.' A doddle, thinks the younger man – 'No way is there a load that you can push that I can't. You're on.'

'All right then,' says Bill, and, indicating the wheelbarrow, adds 'Hop in, lad.'

I Know Him So Well

An elderly couple went to the doctor for their annual medical check-up. The old man went in first, and after he was finished, he waited outside while the doctor examined the old woman.

The doctor said to the wife, 'Before I look at you, I'd like to talk about your husband for a moment. I'm rather concerned about him. I asked him how he was feeling, and he said he felt better than ever. He said that when he got up this morning, he went to the bathroom, opened the door and God turned on the light for him. And when he was done, he said he shut the door and God turned out the light for him. What do you think it means?'

'It means,' sighed the old lady, 'that he's been peeing in the fridge again.'

Wedding Night Nerves

A seventy-seven-year-old man married a girl almost sixty years his junior. As he climbed into bed for the first time with his bride, he said, 'Did your mother tell you what to do on your wedding night?'

'Yes, she told me everything,' replied the girl, kissing him gently.

'Good,' said the elderly gentleman, turning out the light, 'because I've forgotten.'

Blind Date

A man in his sixties agreed to try and fix up his friend from the bowling club with a date, but when the friend was introduced to the woman in question he was horrified.

'She's the ugliest old woman I've ever seen!' he groaned under his breath. 'Her hair's falling out, she's hardly got any teeth, she has a wooden leg and she's only got one eye.'

'I don't know why you're whispering,' said the other man. 'She's deaf, too!'

The Long Walk

Waiting for her elderly husband to arrive home, a woman was alarmed to see a police car pull up outside her house – with her husband in the back seat.

'We found your husband in the park,' the officer explained. 'He said that he was lost and confused and couldn't find his way home.'

'Oh, Henry!' said the wife. 'You've been going to that park for thirty years. How could you get lost?'

Out of the officer's earshot, the husband whispered to his wife, 'I wasn't lost – I was just too tired to walk home.'

Feeling Younger

Two men in their eighties, Bill and Barney, were driving through the countryside when they heard an Ex-Lax commercial on the car radio which ended with the promise: 'It makes you feel young again.'

'We need to get a bottle of that stuff,' Bill said to Barney.

So in the next town they bought a bottle of Ex-Lax, took two tablespoons each and continued on their journey.

A mile further on, Bill said to Barney, 'Well, do you feel younger yet?'

'Not really,' replied Barney.

'No, me neither,' said Bill.

So they pulled over, took four tablespoons of Ex-Lax each and continued on their journey.

A couple of miles later, Bill again asked Barney, 'So do you feel younger yet?'

'No,' said Barney, 'but I've just done a childish thing!'

Sparkling Portrait

A senior woman decided to have her portrait painted. 'Paint me with diamond earrings, a diamond necklace, emerald bracelets and a gold watch,' she ordered the artist.

'But you aren't wearing any of those things,' replied the artist.

'I know,' said the woman. 'It's in case I die before my husband. I'm sure he will remarry right away, and I want his new wife to go crazy looking for the jewellery.'

Last Words

A dying man was lying in his hospital bed hooked up to a ventilator. With his family gathered around the bed, the man gestured desperately for a pen and paper. He then scrawled a brief note before passing away.

His son picked up the scrap of paper and read out the man's last words: 'You're standing on my oxygen tube.'

Hands off the Cookies!

Lying in his room on his deathbed, a man began to smell the aroma of his favourite chocolate chip cookies wafting up the stairs. Summoning his last ounce of energy, he dragged himself from his bed and staggered out of the bedroom. Gripping the hand rail for dear life, he breathlessly made his way down the stairs and into the hall. From there he stumbled into the kitchen and saw half a dozen trays of cookies spread out on a table before him. Seeing this parting gift – a final act of love from his dear, devoted wife – he reached out to take one. But as he did so, he received a hefty whack across the hand from a spatula.

'Leave those alone!' barked his wife. 'They're for the funeral.'

Health Check

Two paramedics were sent to check on an elderly man who had become disorientated. They decided to take him to hospital for closer examination. On the way there, they asked him a few questions in order to ascertain the level of his awareness. Raising their hands simultaneously, they asked him: 'Do you know what we're doing right now?'

The old man slowly looked up, stared out of the ambulance window and said, 'About forty, maybe forty-five.'

Welcome Home

Michael brought his new work colleague, David, home for dinner. As they arrived at the front door, Michael's wife rushed up, threw her arms around her husband and kissed him passionately.

'Wow!' exclaimed David as the wife returned to the kitchen. 'And how long have you two been married?'

'Thirty-five years,' replied Michael.

'You must have a terrific marriage if your wife greets you like that after all these years.'

'Don't be fooled,' said Michael. 'She only does it to make the dog jealous.'

A Last Vacation

As an old man's health failed, his family decided to send him to Florida for two weeks' recuperation by the sea. But as the short break drew to a close, the old man died and his body was shipped back home.

As his family gathered around the open coffin to pay their last respects, one of his nephews commented, 'Doesn't he look wonderful – so at peace with the world?'

'He certainly does,' said a cousin. 'Those two weeks in Palm Beach did him the world of good.'

The Missing Wife

An elderly driver was pulled over by a traffic cop. 'Excuse me, sir,' said the police officer. 'Do you realize that your wife fell out of the car two miles back?'

'Thank goodness,' said the old man. 'I thought I'd gone deaf!'

True Love

On their twenty-fifth wedding anniversary, a wife turned to her husband and said: 'Will you still love me when my hair has gone grey?'
'Why not?' he replied. 'Haven't I loved you through six other colours?'

Worried Sick

An old man went to the doctor and told him that he was suffering from a long list of illnesses – bronchitis, pneumonia, measles, mumps, chicken pox and diphtheria.

'The trouble with you,' said the doctor, 'is that you're a hypochondriac.'

'Oh no!' exclaimed the old man. 'Don't tell me I've got that as well!'

A Changing Man

A middle-aged man went to the doctor for his annual check-up. The nurse asked him how much he weighed, and he replied: 'About 135 pounds.' She then weighed him and the scale read 160.

Next she asked him how tall he was, and he said: 'Five feet eleven inches, I think.' She measured him and revealed that he was only five feet eight.

Then she took his blood pressure and told him that it was too high.

'Of course it's high,' he said. 'When I came in here I was tall and slender. Now I'm short and fat.'

Never Sick

A husband and wife were celebrating their seventieth wedding anniversary, and a newspaper reporter had been sent to cover the occasion.

'You look remarkably healthy for your age,' ventured the reporter.

The wife replied: 'I have never had one day sick in my entire life.'

'So you've never been bedridden?' inquired the reporter.

'Oh, thousands of times!' she said. 'And twice in a golf buggy!'

Misheard Diagnosis

A ninety-two-year-old man went to the doctor for a medical. A few days later, the doctor saw him walking down the street with a beautiful young woman on his arm.

At his follow-up visit, the doctor said to the old man, 'You seem to be having the time of your life.'

'I'm only doing what you said, doctor – "Get a hot momma and be cheerful."'

'I didn't say that at all,' the doctor replied. 'I said: "You've got a heart murmur. Be careful."'

Highway Robbery

A robber held up a stagecoach in America's Mid-West. He snarled: 'If you don't hand over all your money, I'll shoot the men and molest the women.'

A gentleman passenger stepped forward and said bravely, 'You shall not touch the ladies.'

Hearing this, an elderly woman passenger yelled out, 'Leave him alone – *he's* robbing this stagecoach!'

Personal Organizer

Two senior ladies met for the first time since graduating from high school. 'You were always so organized in school. Have you managed to lead a well-planned life?' one asked the other:

'Well, I've been married four times,' said her friend.

'I guess that's not very well-planned.'

'On the contrary. My first marriage was to a millionaire, my second marriage was to an actor, my third marriage was to a preacher, and now I'm married to an undertaker.'

'I don't see what that has to do with a well-planned life.'

'Think about it: one for the money, two for the show, three to get ready, and four to go . . .'

The Church Bells

Saddened by the death of her ninety-year-old grandfather, a young woman went to comfort her grandmother. The girl asked how he had died, and her grandmother replied, 'He had a heart attack Sunday morning while we were making love.'

'Isn't it a little risky having sex at your age?' asked the granddaughter.

'No, not really, my dear. You see, we decided about fifteen years ago that because of our advanced age, we would make love just once a week – and to the sound of the church bells. They are just the right rhythm – nice and slow and even. Nothing too strenuous. They suited our needs perfectly.' She paused to wipe away a tear. 'And your grandfather would still be alive if that ice-cream van hadn't gone past.'

Confusing Signs

A traffic cop pulled over a little old lady for driving too slowly on US Highway 22. 'The speed limit is sixty-five miles per hour on this highway,' he said, 'but you're doing less than twenty-five. How come?'

She explained: 'There are a lot of signs saying twenty-two – that's the speed limit, isn't it? And I was doing twenty-two exactly.'

'No, ma'am, that's not the speed limit, that's the route number.'

'Oh.'

He then glanced in the back of the car and saw two other women. They were white and trembling with fear. 'What's the matter with your passengers?' he asked.

'We've just come off the one marked 126,' the driver replied brightly.

Stuck on the Toilet

A senior lady went to her doctor about her constipation. 'It's terrible,' she said. 'I haven't moved my bowels in more than a week.'

'I see,' said the doctor. 'Have you done anything about it?'

'Oh, yes. I sit in the toilet for at least half an hour in the morning and then again in the evening.'

'No,' said the doctor. 'I mean do you take anything?'

'Of course I do,' she answered. 'I take a magazine.'

Prized Organ

A vicar called on one of his elderly parishioners for afternoon tea. While she was in the kitchen, he admired the beautiful old church organ that was the centrepiece of her lounge. However he was puzzled to see a bowl of water on top of the organ and, even more surprisingly, a condom floating in the water.

When the lady returned with tea and biscuits, the vicar initially refrained from raising the subject of the condom in water, but after a while his curiosity got the better of him.

'Excuse me,' he said, indicating the bowl of water, 'could you tell me what that's all about?'

'Oh, isn't it wonderful!' enthused the old lady. 'I was walking along the street five months ago when I found this little package.

It said to put it on your organ and keep it wet and it would prevent disease. And do you know, it works! I haven't had a cold all winter.'

Deaf Driver

An elderly lady was driving carefully along a motorway. She regularly checked her speed to make sure that she was not exceeding the limit but then, to her dismay, she saw in her rear mirror that a police car was following her, lights flashing.

'What have I done wrong?' she asked herself. 'I'm not speeding, I haven't been drinking, I've got my seat belt on, and the car's just passed its MOT. . .' As she pulled to a halt, she rolled down the window and waited resignedly for the lecture and the inevitable ticket.

The police officer walked up to the window and started speaking but as he did so, the woman pointed to her ear and shook her head, indicating that she was deaf.

The policeman smiled and signed back: 'I know. I'm here to tell you that your horn is stuck!'

A Tear in his Eye

A couple went out to dinner to celebrate their thirtieth wedding anniversary. On their way home, the wife noticed a tear in her husband's eye and wondered if he was getting sentimental about the happy occasion.

'No,' he said, 'I was thinking back to before we got married. Your father threatened me with a shotgun and said he'd have me thrown in jail for thirty years if I didn't marry you. Well, tomorrow I would have been a free man!'

Death of a Spinster

After the death of an aged spinster, her funeral instructions were found among her personal belongings. Along with suggestions for scripture readings and hymns was the following order: 'There will be no male pallbearers. Since they wouldn't take me out when I was alive, I'm not having them take me out when I'm dead.'

Whisky Diet

A woman walked up to a gaunt, wizened little man rocking in a chair outside his front door. 'I couldn't help noticing how contented you look,' she said. 'What's your secret for a long and happy life?'

'I smoke three packs of cigarettes a day, I drink four bottles of whisky a week, and I never take any exercise.'

'That's amazing,' said the woman. 'If you don't mind me asking, how old are you exactly?'

'Thirty-six,' he replied.

No Comment

A census taker knocked on old Miss Wilson's door. She answered all of his questions except one – she flatly refused to tell him her age.

'But,' he protested, 'everyone gives their age to the census taker.'

'Oh yes?' she countered. 'And did Miss Elsie Hill and Miss Nellie Hill tell you their ages?'

'Sure they did,' he replied.

'Well I'm the same age as them.'

So he wrote on his form: 'As old as the Hills.'

The Name Escapes Me

After playing bridge together for many years, two ladies had got to know each other fairly well. Then one afternoon, during a game of cards, one lady looked across to the other and said, 'This is terribly embarrassing, as I realize we've known each other for many years but, for the life of me, I can't remember your husband's name. Would you be so kind as to remind me what it is?'

There was silence for a couple of minutes before the other lady answered, 'How soon do you need to know?'

Buried or Cremated?

A son hesitantly asked his ageing mother, 'I know it's a tricky subject but when you go, would you prefer to be buried or cremated?'

'Oh, I don't really mind,' replied the mother. 'Surprise me!'

A Slap in the Face

A widow was telling her grown-up daughter about a date she had been on with an eighty-eight-year-old man. 'I had to slap his face three times in the course of the evening!'

The daughter was horrified. 'Fancy him getting fresh with you at his age!'

'No, it wasn't that,' explained the mother. 'I had to keep slapping his face to keep him awake.'

Bumpy Landing

The passengers filed off an aeroplane after a bumpy landing. Many were still pale and shaking as the crew said, 'Thank you for flying with us. Hope to see you again soon.'

None of the passengers was brave enough to complain about the traumatic experience until the last person off, a little old lady, said to the flight attendant: 'Tell me, dear, did we land or were we shot down?'

Wall of Death

A funeral was being held for a woman in her seventies. As the pallbearers were carrying out the coffin at the end of the service, they accidentally bumped into a wall. The jolt prompted a groaning sound from within the coffin, and when the lid was opened, amazingly the woman was found to be still alive.

She went on to live for another eleven years before finally dying. At the end of the funeral, the pallbearers again carried out the coffin. As they carried it towards the door, the deceased's husband called out, 'Watch that wall!'

Three Envelopes

Three months after her husband George had died, his widow Gloria finally felt able to reflect on what a kind, considerate man he had been. 'George thought of everything,' she told her friend Martha. 'Just before he died, he called me to his bedside and handed me three envelopes. He said, "I've put all my last requests in these envelopes. After I'm dead, I want you to open them and follow the instructions. Then I shall be able to rest in peace."'

'So what was in the envelopes?' asked Martha eagerly.

'The first envelope contained five thousand pounds along with a note which said: "Please use this money to buy a nice coffin." So I did, and I know that as a result George is resting comfortably,' Gloria told her. 'The second envelope contained ten thousand pounds with a note saying, "Please use this money to give me a good send-off." So I did, and George had the most wonderful funeral. The third envelope contained thirty thousand dollars with a note saying, "Please use this money to buy a nice stone." She held out her hand and pointed to a huge diamond ring. 'You like it?'

A Reliable Doctor

Two elderly men were arguing the merits of their respective doctors. 'I don't trust your fancy doctor,' said one. 'He treated Jed Pilbeam for ten months for a kidney complaint and then poor old Jed died of a liver ailment.'

'So what makes you think your doctor is any better?'

'Because when my doctor treats you for a kidney complaint, you can be sure you'll die of a kidney complaint!'

Acute Angina

An elderly woman was admitted to hospital with a mystery illness. After monitoring her for two days, the doctor told her, 'You have acute angina.'

'Oh, doctor,' said the old woman blushing, 'you do say the sweetest things!'

Little White Lie

To the envy of his friends, a sixty-nine-year-old millionaire married a twenty-year-old model. 'You lucky devil!' said one. 'How did you manage to land such a beautiful young wife?'

'Easy,' replied the millionaire. 'I told her I was ninety-six.'

Dog's Tail

A middle-aged man took his dog to the vet and asked him to cut off the dog's tail.

'Why do you want to do that?' asked the vet. 'His tail is perfectly healthy.'

'I know,' said the man. 'But my wife's Great-Aunt Gladys is arriving tomorrow, and I don't want anything to make her think she is welcome.'

A True Gentleman

On his retirement, a widower decided to travel around the world. While journeying through the American Mid-West, he found himself stranded in a small town which had only one hotel. Although the standard of accommodation was not quite what he was used to, he had no option but to knock on the door and ask whether the hotel could put him up for the night.

'Sorry, we don't have any spare rooms tonight,' said the manager, 'but I guess you could share with a little red-headed schoolteacher.'

The widower's eyes lit up in anticipation. 'Yes, that would be fine,' he said, adding, 'And don't worry, I'll be a real gentleman.'

'Just as well,' said the manager. 'So will the little red-headed schoolteacher.'

Taking Leave of his Census

An old timer was sitting on the porch of his Maine farmhouse when a young man approached holding a pen and a clipboard.

'What are you selling, son?' he asked.

'I'm not selling anything. I'm the census taker.'

'Oh no you're not!'

'Sir?'

'You're not taking mine ... they'll put me in a home then.'

'Ah – no, no! We're just trying to find out how many people there are in the United States.'

'Well, you're wasting your time with me,' said the old man. 'I got no idea.'

Trip to Jerusalem

A long-suffering husband and his wife went on holiday to Jerusalem, but while they were there, the wife died. The local undertaker told the husband: 'You can have her shipped home for 16,000 shekels or you can have her buried here in the Holy Land for 800 shekels.'

After a moment's thought, the husband said, 'I think I'll have her shipped home.'

'Well, it's your decision,' said the undertaker, 'but I must say I'm surprised. Why spend 16,000 shekels on having your wife shipped back to Britain when for just 800 you could have her buried right here?'

'Listen,' said the husband. 'Many years ago, a man died here, was buried here, and three days later he rose from the dead. I just can't take that risk.'

Walking Economy

An old man was walking along the street with a younger friend. As they passed a news stand he indicated the newspaper headlines, which were all about the current financial crisis, to his companion and remarked, 'That's me.'

'What do you mean?'

'My hair line is in recession, my shoulders are slumped, my stomach is a victim of inflation, my prospects are gloomy and the combination of these factors is putting me into a deep depression.'

The Safe Option

A wife took her elderly husband tenderly by the hand and whispered in his ear: 'Tonight I'm going to give you super sex.'

'Sounds wonderful,' he said. 'I'll have the soup.'

Erratic Driving

A police officer stopped a car on a quiet country road and walked up to the elderly lady driver. 'Excuse me, madam,' he said, 'but can you explain why you have been driving so erratically? You were weaving all over the road.'

'Thank goodness you're here, officer,' she gasped. 'I almost had an accident. I looked up and there was a tree right in front of me. I swerved to the left and there was another tree. So I swerved to the right and there was another tree. I was absolutely terrified.'

Calmly the officer reached through the side window to the rear-view mirror and grasped the object that was hanging down beside it. 'Madam, there was no tree. It was your air freshener.'

Far-Sighted

An old man was a witness in a robbery case. The defence lawyer asked him, 'Did you see my client commit this robbery?'

'Yes, I did,' said the old man.

'Can you be absolutely certain that it was my client?' continued the lawyer. 'Let's not forget, the robbery took place at night.'

'I'm definitely sure it was him,' said the old man. 'I got a good look at him.'

'You may think you did,' persisted the lawyer, 'but you are eighty one years old and the suspect was standing on the other side of the street. Just exactly how far can you see – particularly at night?'

'Well,' replied the old man. 'I can see the moon. Is that far enough for you?'

Senior Personal Ads

MEMORIES: I can usually remember Monday through Thursday. If you can remember Friday, Saturday and Sunday, let's put our heads together.

SERENITY NOW: I'm into solitude, long walks and meditation. If you are the silent type, let's get together, take our hearing aids out and enjoy quiet times.

LONG-TERM COMMITMENT: Widow who has recently buried her fourth husband looking for someone to complete a six-unit plot. High blood pressure, coronary problems and blackouts not a problem.

WINNING SMILE: Active grandmother with original teeth seeking a dedicated flosser to share rare steaks, corn on the cob, Rolos, etc.

FOXY LADY: Fashion-conscious, blue-haired beauty, slim, 5'4' (used to be 5'6'), searching for sharp-dressing companion. No soup stains on tie please.

MINT CONDITION: Male, 1932, high mileage, good condition, some hair, many new parts including hip, knee, cornea, valves. Isn't in running condition, but walks well.

You Can't Take It With You

A mean-spirited old miser diagnosed with a terminal illness was determined to prove wrong the saying 'You can't take it with you.' So he ordered his long-suffering wife to go to the bank and withdraw enough money to fill two pillowcases. He then told her to place the cash-filled pillowcases in the attic directly above his bed, reasoning that when he died, he would grab the money on his way up to heaven.

The ever-obedient wife followed the instructions to the letter.

Several weeks after his death, she was cleaning the attic when she came across the pillowcases still filled with cash. 'The silly old fool!' she said to herself. 'I knew he should have told me to put the money in the basement!'

Holding Hands

A pastor was touched to see a couple of his senior parishioners holding hands throughout his Sunday service. Afterwards he said to them, 'In this day and age where divorce is rife, it is so refreshing to see two people who have been married for over forty years still being openly affectionate towards one another. To hold hands through the entire service, it must be true love.'

'It's not love, pastor,' said the wife. 'It's to stop him from cracking his knuckles!'

Mother's Boy

A man in his fifties still living at his parents' home told his overbearing mother that he had finally fallen in love and was going to get married. 'I'm going to bring three women over to the house tomorrow night,' he said, 'and you, Mother, have to guess which one I'm going to marry.'

'If I must,' muttered the mother miserably.

The following evening the son ushered three attractive women into the living room and asked them to sit down.

'Now,' he asked his mother, 'which one do you think is the woman that I'm going to marry?'

'The one in the middle,' replied the mother without hesitation.

'That's right!' he exclaimed. 'How did you know?'
'Because I don't like her.'

Waiting for God

After years of regularly going to church, a man in his late nineties suddenly stopped attending. When the vicar saw him in the street, he asked why the man had decided to change the habit of a lifetime.

The old man whispered, 'When I got to eighty-five, I expected God to take me any day. But then I got to ninety, ninety-five, and now ninety-seven. So I thought God is obviously a very busy man and must have forgotten about me, and I really don't want to remind him!'

A Mind of His Own

Everybody on Earth died and went to Heaven. On their arrival, God announced that he wanted the men to form two lines – one for all the men who had dominated their women on Earth, the other for all the men who had been dominated by their women. Then he instructed the women to go with St Peter.

When God turned around, he saw that the men had indeed formed two lines. The line of men who had been dominated by their women stretched back over a hundred miles whereas the line of men who had dominated their women consisted of just one person – a balding little man in his sixties.

God was livid. 'You men should be ashamed of yourselves for having been so spineless! Only one of my sons has been strong. He is the only man of whom I am truly proud.'

God then addressed the little man who was standing alone. 'Tell me, my noble son, how did you manage to be the only one in this line?'

'I'm not sure,' he replied meekly. 'My wife told me to stand here.'

Crowded Bus

An elderly man boarded a crowded bus but nobody would give him a seat. When the bus jerked away, the old man's walking stick slipped and he fell to the floor. As he got to his feet, a boy of about nine or ten sitting nearby said to him, 'If you put a little rubber thing on the end of your stick, it wouldn't slip.'

The old man replied, 'Yes, sonny, and if your dad had done the same thing nine years ago, I'd have a bloody seat today!'

A Calculating Husband

A middle-aged wife bought a selection of cosmetics designed to knock years off her age. After spending six hours carefully applying the various creams and potions, she asked her husband, 'Tell me honestly, darling, how old do you think I look?'

The husband replied: 'From your skin, twenty-three; from your hair, nineteen; from your figure, twenty-two.'

'Oh, you flatterer!' she gushed.

'Wait a minute,' he said. 'I haven't added them up yet.'

Healthy Move

At the suggestion of his doctor, an elderly man retired to live in the country. On his second day in his new home, he met his neighbour who was also in his seventies. 'My doctor told me this would be a healthy place to live,' said the man. 'Is that true?'

'It certainly is,' replied the neighbour. 'Why, when I first arrived here, I couldn't say a single word, I had hardly any hair on my head, I didn't have the strength to walk across a room, and I had to be lifted in and out of bed.'

'That's an amazing transformation,' said the man. 'How long have you lived here?'

'I was born here,' said the neighbour.

Hot for her Husband

A couple were sitting at the breakfast table on the morning of their golden wedding anniversary. The husband said to the wife, 'Just think, we've been married fifty years.'

'Yes,' she replied. 'Fifty years ago today, we were sitting at this same breakfast table.'

'I know,' he said, 'and what's more, if my memory serves me right, we were stark naked!'

'Oh!' she giggled. 'What do you say we get naked again for old times' sake?'

So they stripped off and sat down naked at the breakfast table.

'Honey,' gasped the old lady breathlessly, 'I have to tell you, my breasts are as hot for you today as they were fifty years ago.'

'I'm not surprised,' he answered. 'One's in your coffee and the other is in your porridge!'

Auntie Goes For a Walk

An elderly lady from the country went to visit her niece and husband in a fashionable city suburb. Nearby was a smart golf course.

On the second afternoon of her visit, the old lady went for a stroll and on her return, the niece asked, 'Well, Auntie, did you enjoy yourself?'

'Yes,' said Auntie. 'Before I had walked very far, I came to some beautiful rolling fields. There were a number of people about, mostly men. Some of them kept shouting at me in a very eccentric manner, but I took no notice. Four men followed me for some time, shouting something I couldn't understand and waving what looked like big sticks. Naturally I ignored them, too.

'Oh, and by the way,' she added, holding out her hands, 'I found a number of these strange little white balls, so I picked them all up and brought them home, hoping that you could explain to me what they mean.'

Serial Widow

Two spinsters – Ethel and Mabel – were talking in a nursing home. Ethel said: 'Martha has just cremated her fifth husband.'

'I guess that's the way it goes,' said Mabel. 'Some of us can't find a husband, and others have husbands to burn.'

A Real Catch

Two widows, Joan and Gloria, were eager to learn more about the distinguished gentleman who had just moved into their exclusive apartment block. One day Gloria said to Joan, 'You know how shy I am, Joan. Why don't you ambush him at the pool and find out all you can about him? He looks so lonely.'

So Joan went over to talk to the man as he sat beside the pool. 'My friend and I were wondering why you look so lonely,' she said.

'Of course I'm lonely,' he answered. 'I've spent the last eighteen years in prison.'

'Oh, why?'

'I strangled my third wife.'

'Oh. What happened to your second wife?'

'I shot her.'

'And what about your first wife?'

'We had a fight and she fell from the tenth floor of our block.'

'Oh, my!' Joan then turned to her friend on the other side of the pool and called out: 'Yoo-hoo, Gloria! It's okay. He's single.'

Fitness Freak

Boasting about his fitness to a group of youngsters, an elderly man said, 'Every morning, I do fifty push-ups, fifty sit-ups, and I walk three miles. In fact, I bet I'm fitter than any of you. You know why? I don't smoke, I don't drink, I don't stay up late, and I don't chase after women. And tomorrow I'm going to celebrate my eighty-eighth birthday!'

'Really?' said one of the youngsters. 'How?'

The Biter Bit

Two ladies 'of a certain age' – Clarissa and Eleanor – who were rivals in their social circle, met for a Christmas lunch at a country club.

'My dear,' said Clarissa, 'are those real pearls?'

'They certainly are,' replied Eleanor.

'Of course,' smiled Clarissa, 'the only way I could tell for sure would be to bite them.'

'Yes,' said Eleanor, 'but to do that you would need real teeth.'

Forgotten Glasses

A couple in their sixties went for a drive into the country and stopped for lunch at one of their favourite restaurants. After lunch, they had driven about twelve miles when the woman suddenly remembered that she had left her glasses at the restaurant. Her husband was cross at having to go back for them. 'How could you forget your glasses?' he moaned. 'This will add nearly an hour to the journey. The whole day is going to be wasted!'

He was still complaining when they pulled up outside the restaurant. As his wife got out of the car, he grumbled, 'I suppose while you're in there, you may as well get my hat, too.'

Roadside Shock

A juggler was driving to a show when he was pulled over by a police officer who became suspicious on discovering matches and lighter fuel in the glove compartment.

'What are these for?' he asked.

'I'm a juggler,' replied the driver.

'Oh yes?' said the officer. 'Let's see you prove it.'

So the driver collected his props and started to juggle three blazing torches at the roadside.

Just then an elderly couple drove by. The husband turned to his wife and said, 'I'm really glad I quit drinking. Look at the test they're giving now!'

The Great Dictator

An elderly man approached a teenager in the post office. 'Excuse me, young man,' he said. 'Could I possibly ask you to address this postcard for me because my arthritis is terrible today and I can hardly hold a pen?'

'Yes, okay,' said the young man, and he wrote down the address given to him.

'Also,' added the old man, 'would you be so kind as to write a brief message on the card and sign it in my name?'

'Okay,' said the young man, and he patiently wrote the five-line message that the old man dictated to him, adding his name at the end. Then helpfully he asked, 'Is there anything else you need?'

'There is one thing,' replied the old man. 'After my name, could you just add: "PS: Please excuse the sloppy handwriting."'

Sex Drive

An eighty-one-year-old man went to the doctor and said: 'Doctor, my sex drive is too high. I want it lowered.'

'Am I hearing you right?' asked the doctor, dumbfounded. 'You're eighty-one and you want your sex drive *lowered*?'

'That's right,' said the old man, pointing to his head. 'It's all up here at the moment. I want it lowered.'

The Three Pairs
A young girl wondered why her grandfather needed three pairs of glasses.
'I have one pair for long sight,' he explained to her, 'one pair for short sight, and the third pair to look for the other two.'

Read the Label

A man arrived home from work and noticed that his father seemed to be avoiding the grandchildren. 'What's the problem?' he asked. 'You usually love playing with them.'

The old man produced a medicine prescription from his pocket and said, 'Read the label. That's why!'

The son took the bottle and read the label: 'Take two pills a day. KEEP AWAY FROM CHILDREN.'

Purely Academic

Two elderly academics – one a retired history professor, the other a retired professor of psychology – had been persuaded by their wives to take a week's holiday on Spain's Costa del Sol. As they sat in their shorts on the hotel balcony one balmy evening sipping glasses of wine, the history professor turned to the psychology professor and said: 'Have you read Marx?'

'Yes,' answered the professor of psychology. 'I think it must be these wicker chairs.'

A Lesson Learned

A mother decided one Christmas that she was no longer going to remind her children to write thank-you notes after receiving presents. As a result their grandfather never received any thanks for the generous cheques he had given them.

But the following year things were different. 'All the kids came over personally to thank me,' beamed Grandad.

'That's great,' said the mother. 'But why do you think they decided to change their behaviour?'

'It's obvious,' said Grandad. 'This year I didn't sign the cheques!'

Everything Shared

A young man was studying an elderly couple in McDonald's. He saw that they had ordered one meal and an extra drinks cup. Then he watched the old man carefully cut the hamburger in half, divide the fries into two equal portions, pour half of the soft drink into the extra cup, and start to eat.

Touched by their obvious poverty, the young man asked if he could buy them another meal so that they didn't have to split everything in two.

'Oh, no,' said the old man, 'this is the way we do things. We've been married for nearly sixty years, and we always share everything.'

The young man asked the woman if she was going to eat.

'Not yet,' she replied. 'It's his turn with the teeth.'

The Offer

An elderly lady walked into the recreation room of a nursing home. Holding her clenched fist in the air, she announced, 'Anyone who can guess what's in my hand can have sex with me right now.'

An old man called out in a bored voice, 'An elephant.'

'Near enough!' she said, and dragged him off to her room.

A Rose by Any Other Name

Having become forgetful in their old age, a couple tried to improve their memory by attending special classes where they were taught to remember things by means of word association.

The husband was telling his neighbour how helpful the classes had been.

'Who was the instructor?' asked the neighbour.

'Oh, uh, what was the name now?' mused the husband. 'What's that flower that smells nice and has thorns?'

'A rose?'

'That's it!' exclaimed the husband. He then turned towards the house and called, 'Hey, Rose, what's the name of the guy in charge of the memory class?'

Delayed Reaction

Bert and George were sitting in the park watching a pretty girl walk by. Bert turned to George and said, 'Do you remember those bromide pills they gave us in the war to stop us chasing after women?'

'Yes,' said George. 'What about them?'

Bert said, 'I think mine are beginning to work.'

Missing Husband

A woman went to the police to report her husband missing. She said, 'He's fifty-one, six foot three inches tall, dark eyes, dark hair, athletic build, weighs 185 pounds, smartly dressed and softly spoken.'

'He's five foot two inches, overweight, bald, scruffy and has a big mouth!' her friend protested.

'I know,' said the wife. 'But who wants *him* back?'

No Arguments

To mark her one hundredth birthday, a woman was interviewed by a local newspaper reporter who asked her the secret of her longevity.

'It's easy,' she said. 'My motto has always been to avoid arguments at all costs. I never argue with anybody.'

The reporter was sceptical. 'There must be some other explanation – plenty of exercise, a sensible diet, genetics perhaps? I can't believe you have lived to a hundred simply by not arguing!'

The old woman said: 'You know, you could be right.'

Crossed Wires

Two widows were sitting drinking tea and talking about their late husbands. One turned to the other and said, 'Did you have mutual orgasms?'

'No, I think we were with the Prudential.'

Nightly Routines

Three men in their sixties were discussing their lives.

One said, 'I'm still a once-a-night man.'

The second said, 'Well, I'm a twice-a-night man.'

The third said, 'My wife will tell you that I'm a five-times-a-night man.'

And they all agreed: 'We really shouldn't drink so much tea before we go to bed.'

A Simple Explanation

An elderly couple went for their annual medical. After thoroughly examining the husband, the doctor said, 'I'm pleased to say you seem to be in remarkably good health for someone of your age. Do you have any concerns at all?'

'There is one thing,' said the old man. 'After I have sex with my wife for the first time, I'm usually hot and sweaty. But after I have sex with her for the second time, I usually feel cold and shivery.'

'I see,' said the doctor. 'It's not a complaint I'm familiar with, so I'll have to look into it. I'll let you know what I find out.'

Then the doctor examined the wife. After giving her the usual tests, he said, 'You seem to be in excellent health. Do you have any concerns at all?'

'No, not really, doctor.'

'Oh, because your husband mentioned that whenever he has sex with you for the first time, he feels hot and sweaty, but after he has sex with you for the second time, he feels cold and shivery. Have you any idea what might be causing this?'

'The silly old fool!' said the wife. 'It's because the first time we have sex is usually in July and the second time is usually in December!'

Passing the Time

An old man was sitting on a train, mumbling to himself, smiling, and then raising his hand. After a few moments of silence, he would go through the same routine all over again – mumbling, smiling, raising his hand, silence.

A woman passenger sitting opposite observed this unusual behaviour for some time before her curiosity finally got the better of her. 'Excuse me, sir,' she said. 'Is anything wrong?'

'Oh, no,' replied the old man. 'It's just that long train trips get boring, so to pass the time I tell myself jokes.'

'That explains the mumbling and the smiling,' said the woman, 'but why do you also raise your hand?'

'Ah,' said the old man, 'that's to interrupt myself because I've heard that one before.'

Senility Prayer

God grant me the senility to forget the people I never liked anyway, the good fortune to run into the ones I do, and the eyesight to tell the difference.